THE COMING KING

A Growing Theological Controversy

R. Baruch Ph.D.

Areli Media

The Coming King

The Growing Controversy about the Millennial Kingdom and
the Coming Reign of Messiah
by R. Baruch Ph.D.

ISBN 10: 996244107
ISBN 13: 978-0-9962441-0-7

eISBN 10: 996244115
eISBN 13: 978-0-9962441-1-4

Published by Areli Media
www.AreliMedia.com

To my wife Rivka,
who has demonstrated her love for me beyond
what any husband could expect.

CONTENTS

PREFACE

When one sets out on any theological pursuit, his primary set of instructions must be the Word of G-d. One's view of Scripture is paramount in assuring that he arrives at the right destination—Truth! If a person properly views Scripture as the divine utterance of G-d, verbally inspired and without error; then this one, with the Holy Spirit to guide him, has the greatest likelihood of achieving a correct understanding of G-d's revelation. Because of the great importance of Scripture in forming a correct theological perspective, all the Biblical citations which appear in this book, have been carefully translated from the original languages by the author in a very literal manner. Where necessary, he provides an additional translation to assists the reader in gaining the proper intent of the verse or verses.

The purpose of this book is to guide the reader through the primary Biblical texts associated with the Millennial Kingdom. When a person understands the events which will take place during the Millennium, he will gain a greater appreciation for the faithfulness of G-d. Throughout this book, the term "*HaShem*" is frequently used when referring to the L-rd. This word literally means, "The *Name*" and is commonly used by the Jewish community when speaking about G-d. The use of this term is for the purpose of showing the greatest respect to our L-rd and is rooted in obedience to the commandment, not to lift up the name of the L-rd in vain.

When one examines the primary texts relating to the Millennial Kingdom, this person will soon learn that Israel, both the Jewish people and the Land of, figure significantly in this Kingdom. Although Scriptural revelation provides the reader with a clear presentation of this Kingdom, many theologians have chosen to discount the plain meaning of those texts, and in turn offer allegorical and highly spiritualized understandings of these passages. Such a methodology is flawed and forces those theologians to ignore much of the prophetic record or to interpret them in a manner that is in opposition to the stated purpose of the prophet. There is another consequence of such a methodology.

An important aspect of the Scriptures is the continuity between the Old and New Covenants. When one properly understands the revelation concerning the Millennial Kingdom, it actually enhances a person's ability to perceive the close and inherent continuity between the covenants. One learns that the central messages that began in the opening chapters of the book of Genesis and continued throughout the Old Testament became the same messages which are found throughout the New Testament.

Among the many aspects related to the Millennial Kingdom is the clear demonstration that the Torah, which HaShem gave to Israel at Mount Sinai, provided the basis whereby one could understand the righteous will of G-d. It will be during the Millennium that Israel will obey the Torah and lead the nations to follow in this obedience which will manifest the righteousness of G-d and cause His blessings to be experienced by all who submit to His laws. For most Christians, this concept is foreign and may appear to be in conflict with what they have learned. However, when one is diligent and he or she honestly studies the Scriptures, they will find a consistency between the purposes and plans of G-d found in His revelation at Mount Sinai and the teachings of Messiah Yeshua.

INTRODUCTION

When the word "Kingdom" is mentioned, what enters into one's mind? Obviously the answer to this question depends on who is asked. Traditionally, Judaism would portray the Kingdom as a monarchy under the rule of an anointed king from the city of Jerusalem. Judaism would also understand that the Land of Israel and the Jewish people would figure largely into this Kingdom, having authority over all the other nations. Christianity, on the other hand, emphasizes by and large, a heavenly rule of Messiah rather than that of an earthly reign. The Christian view also, to an increasing degree, diminishes Israel's role in the Kingdom and does not see the Land of Israel or the Jewish people as having any special significance in the Kingdom. Also, Christianity in general, understands the Kingdom in more spiritual terms where most of the natural elements of this age are done away with. Are these differences based upon what is written in the T'nach (Old Testament) or that which is found in the New Testament? Is it possible to reconcile the Kingdom message found in both Testaments and arrive at a Scriptural view of the Kingdom of G-d? This is the primary task of this study.

Part of the divergent views in regard to the issue of the Kingdom is the reality that there are clearly two different, but related, Kingdoms revealed in the Bible. The first is commonly referred to as the Millennial Kingdom, while the second is known as the New Jerusalem. Much of the confusion concerning this issue of the Kingdom is caused when one fails to make a proper distinction between these two Kingdoms. This book, however, will only deal with the Millennial Kingdom, which is rightly defined as the thousand year rule of Messiah Yeshua (Jesus) from Jerusalem over the entire world. This book will not discuss in detail those events which will bring about the Millennial Kingdom; rather it will primarily focus on what will occur during these thousand years and the theological implications which are associated with the Millennial Kingdom.

Theologians hold different views concerning the Millennial Kingdom. The views are usually based on and highly influenced by a particular theologian's understanding of the inspiration and authority of Scripture. In order to distinguish between these different views, it is common to relate these various perspectives in terms of Messiah's return. For example, one view holds that Yeshua will return prior to the establishment of the Millennial Kingdom. This view is known as **Pre-millennialism**. Another view holds to the belief that Messiah's return is after the completion of the Millennial Kingdom. This is known as **Post-millennialism**. There is an additional view known as **Amillennialism**, which denies the existence of a Millennial Kingdom altogether. Those who hold to a literal interpretation of Scripture, and strong continuity between the Old and New Testaments, usually embrace the Pre-millennial view. The vast majority of this book will deal with a Pre-millennial perspective. However, it is necessary before delving into this view, that some discussion of the other two views be presented.

Amillennialism and Post-millennialism

Amillennialism asserts that there will be no Millennial Kingdom, i.e. no physical rule of Messiah from the city of Jerusalem. It is vital that the reader be aware that there are major similarities between aspects of the Amillennial view and that of the Post-millennial view. Although there are indeed technical differences between these two perspectives, it is not necessary that such differences be detailed in this study to any significant manner. When examining the general conclusions of these two perspectives, it seems that they are enough similar for our purposes that it is not required to present them separately. For example, in regard to the reign of Messiah on earth, Post-millennialism asserts that this rule is occurring now through Messiah's followers. Post-millennialists base their view on the fact that Scripture states that believers are the body of Messiah. The question that needs to be asked is whether it is correct to assert that the Church rules over the earth today? Obviously for those who would answer in the affirmative, their position would be based in a highly symbolic and spiritualized understanding of this issue, so that the reality of the situation is far removed.

Amillennialism holds that the Scriptural passages that deal with Yeshua's reign on earth should be understood as symbolic, rather than literal. Hence, whether Messiah rules through His followers (Post-millenialism) or whether one understands His rule as only symbolic, the implications are the same; namely, Messiah Yeshua does **not** reign physically and literally from the city of Jerusalem. The manner in which Amillennialists handle the primary texts dealing with the Millennial Kingdom reveals a manner of Biblical interpretation that, when applied to other Scriptures, provides a basis for theological perspectives which are far from the acceptable norms. Please understand that generally speaking, Amillennialists may not accept such theological positions, but their methodology for Biblical interpretation in regard to the Millennium opens the door for these heresies to find a foothold within Christianity. It then becomes difficult for them to argue against these problematic theological perspectives when they were derived from the same errant methodology.

It is also important to note that since Messiah's ascension back into the heavens, more than a thousand years have passed; hence Post-millennialists are now forced to interpret the thousand years as not a literal period of a thousand years as the word of G-d states, but simply as an undefined period of time. It is also important to note that Post-millenialists state that prior to Messiah's coming, the Gospel must be successfully preached and received by the nations and become the ruling standard in the world. Therefore it is hard to believe that the world is anywhere close to the end of this age. Due to this belief, Post-millennialists understand much of the book of Revelation, which deals with judgment and tribulation, to be referring to the past. They also apply this perspective to the vast majority of other Biblical prophecies.

Amillennialists on the other hand, do not need to deny an end of the age which contains tribulation and judgment, yet most Amillennialists prefer to hold to Messiah's coming at any moment and therefore do not see any signs or events necessary which must take place prior to His return. In reality, a good percentage of Amillennialists share the Post-millennial view that the preaching of the Gospel will be highly successful and a period of general peace and prosperity will precede Messiah's return.

The key tendency of both perspectives is to hold to a reluctance to interpret Scripture according to its plain and simple meaning. Rather, there is a preference to allegorize and spiritualize Scripture, especially as previously mentioned, Old Testament prophecy. In reality, for both of these groups prophecy holds a position of lesser significance than that of the New Testament. What is emphasized by these two views is a belief that through the lens of "faith" (in Messiah) one is able to interpret Scripture in a superior manner. There is no question that faith in Messiah provides the key element in properly interpreting Scripture. However, if one arrives at an understanding of a particular text, which is in conflict with the clear meaning of other Biblical texts, then it should be obvious that the so-called "lens of faith" contains a serious flaw. A good example of this problem is illustrated by the Middle East conflict between the Israelis and the Palestinians.

It is very common for Amillennialists and Post-Millennialists to assert an allegiance with the Palestinians rather than with the Israelis. The primary reason for this is because they perceive the "plight" of the Palestinians to be the more "righteous" cause. Their rationale is based on the perception that because Messiah Yeshua was often moved with compassion for those who were suffering, and today the media often presents news stories of Palestinians suffering; then Messiah would most certainly be on the side of the Palestinians. There are some serious flaws with such a position. First, it is incorrect to believe that Yeshua always acted on behalf of the one whose suffering was to the greater extent. What concerned Him was justice, and justice is rooted in Scriptural truth. In other words, it is wrong to assume or to assert that the righteous cause is always with the one who is the weaker of the two, or the one who is suffering more. Even though the Palestinians are weaker than the Israelis, one must never forget that the L-rd (HaShem) has given the Land of Israel to the Jewish people and it is the Palestinians who are standing against the Biblically stated will of G-d.

Secondly, one must always identify the source of the suffering. In this example, there is an overwhelming media bias against the Israelis, which asserts that the cause of the Palestinian suffering is at the hands of the Israeli government alone; while failing to acknowledge that the true cause of this suffering is the Islamic teachings that encourage terrorism and fail to do much to provide or even allow an environment for economic development. Clearly, it is the objectives of the Palestinian leadership which have led to a forfeit of opportunities that would provide a higher quality of life for those they govern, that is the cause of its people's suffering. Israel is simply acting to preserve her security requirements. Obviously much more could be written on this issue, but for the purpose of this book, it is only necessary to demonstrate that the hermeneutical approach, which interprets Scripture with broad theological sweeps based in some general views of Messiah Yeshua, and without doing a thorough study of all matters related to the text or issue, is the one that can actually arrive at conclusions which are at variance with proper theological positions.

There is another dangerous aspect of this methodology. As was previously stated, both Amillennialists and Post-millennialists claim that the character of Messiah, **as they understand it**, provides the proper "lens of faith" for interpreting the Scriptures. Such a subjective view tends to ignore key hermeneutical indicators located in the Biblical text, and can actually give rise to a type of "Gnosticism." In the end, this "lens of faith" approach offers interpretations which are in reality against the plans and purposes of the Messiah. As has been stated by many others, Gnosticism, which values subjective and personal understandings of theological matters above painstaking efforts of sound exegetical methodology, will lead to heresy, rather than those truths which will exalt Yeshua and manifest His superiority.

Millennial Views and Israel

In a similar way, where Messiah's return helps define one's perspective concerning the Millennial Kingdom, so too is one's view of Israel paramount in presenting a theological framework for understanding this Kingdom. Both Amillennialists and Post-millennialists tend not to see any unique role for Israel in the last days or in the Millennial Kingdom. Many either understand that the Church has replaced Israel as G-d's covenant people, or Israel is a rebel nation who has forsaken her special call altogether, and therefore the purposes which the L-rd had once offered to her are now rendered void.

As Amillennialism grows among Evangelicals, some do see that in the last days a great number of Jewish individuals will come to faith. However, despite this apparent return to G-d by the Jewish people in a unique manner, **they** strongly reject the view that Israel will have a leading role, or for that matter any real significance, in any future epochs. Rather, **they** assert that these new Jewish believers are simply absorbed into the Church. Again, it must be stated that for **Amillennialists** and **Post-Millenialists** too, it is only the Church that holds any role in G-d's future plans and purposes. **They** allow for the view that the Jewish people are invited to become part of the Church as all other people are invited, and even if many should respond in the last days, it does not represent for **them** any significant purpose unique to the Jewish people, nor does this occurrence foreshadow any behavior of G-d based on covenant promises He made to Israel. For **them** the covenant has been entirely canceled out.

Since most evangelicals place this spiritual awakening as taking place after the Rapture, it would therefore be **incorrect** to say that these Jewish believers, and for that matter those Gentiles, who come to faith after the Rapture are simply absorbed into the Church. The reason why this is incorrect is because these new believers will not have received a glorified new body and therefore there will be a great distinction between them and those who took part in the Rapture, i.e. the Church. It is this distinction that actually assists one in understanding who will be present at the beginning of the Millennial Kingdom and the unique role that each of these various groups will possess.

Chapter 1

THE KINGDOM PLAYERS

Once again, it is vital for the reader to understand that those events which will bring about the Millennial Kingdom are not the primary focus of this book. However, in this first chapter, some of those events, as well as the instructions that Messiah gave concerning this transitional period known as the last days, will be discussed. The reason for doing so is to demonstrate the important role that Israel will have in establishing the Millennial Kingdom. The rest of this book, however, will deal with the thousand years from Messiah's return to the Mount of Olives, up to the release of Satan at the end of the thousand years. It is significant that when Messiah Yeshua returns to establish the Kingdom, He will appear on the Mount of Olives, exactly as it was promised in Acts chapter 1,

> "And these ones said, 'Men of Galilee, why have you stood looking into the heavens, this Yeshua has been taken up from you into the heavens, this One will come in the manner you have seen Him go into the heavens.'"
>
> Acts 1:11

Although this verse only says that Yeshua will return from the heavens in the same manner He ascended, it is significant that He ascended from the Mount of Olives. When one places this verse alongside of Zechariah's revelation in chapter 14, it becomes clear that Yeshua will indeed return from the heavens and arrive at the Mount of Olives to inaugurate the Millennial Kingdom.

> *"And His feet will stand on that day upon the Mount of Olives which is before Jerusalem on the East..."*
>
> Zechariah 14:4

Why does Yeshua return from the heavens to the Mount of Olives, rather than to some other location in or around Jerusalem? Today the Mount of Olives contains a large cemetery. Why would this location become the most significant Jewish burial place in the world? The answer is related to the information which is provided in various Biblical texts. It is possible to summarize this information with one word— comfort. When the word comfort is said, what enters into one's thoughts? A common response is a fulfillment of a promise or promises. Death is seen by many as an end or termination to one's life and therefore it is viewed as a destroyer of hope. As it is recorded in Isaiah,

> *"...For Sheol will not give thanks to You, nor will death praise You; **the ones who descend to the pit do not hope for Your faithfulness.**"*
>
> Isaiah 38:18

In reality, death is not the end of hope for those who believe in the message of the Messiah. The Jewish community understood that Messiah's coming is related to the establishment of His Kingdom and ultimately it is in this Kingdom that HaShem's promises to Israel and to the world will be fulfilled. Hence, it is the return of Messiah which offers hope and therefore comforts even the dead. Therefore, it should not be surprising that in the exact location where Scripture reveals Messiah will return, a Jewish cemetery was established.

This point raises a puzzling question. If the Kingdom relates to the fulfillment of so many of G-d's promises, then why is it that so many believers in Yeshua as the Messiah know so little concerning the Kingdom? In fact, when confronted with many of the passages that relate to the Kingdom, the vast majority of believers are unable to articulate a coherent explanation of how these various passages work together to reveal what the Millennial Kingdom will be like.

Although many different aspects of the Kingdom will be presented in this book, the first thing that needs to be addressed is who will populate the Millennial Kingdom? Although the answer varies somewhat with time, let us begin with the first day of the Millennium, the very day when Yeshua's feet will land on the Mount of Olives, and the time of tribulation and judgment is over. There will be three groups who will populate the Millennial Kingdom on day one. They are:

1. Believers who took part in the Rapture.

2. Jewish individuals who came to faith after the Rapture.

3. Gentile individuals who came to faith after the Rapture.

Please notice that the Rapture plays a critical role in defining each group. The Rapture speaks of a Scriptural event which relates to **all believers**, both those who have died in faith and those who are still living at the time when Messiah will summon His followers (both dead and alive) to meet Him in the sky in order for Him to fulfill a very special and key promise relating to the Kingdom. In essence, the Rapture is when Yeshua will depart from the heavens with the command of the archangel and the sound of the Shofar (ram's horn), and call those who belong to Him to ascend into the sky where they will meet Him and receive their new bodies, then return with Him into the heavens (See First Thessalonians 4:16-18 and First Corinthians 15:35-58). However, when Yeshua returns to Jerusalem in order to inaugurate His Kingdom, so too will this first group be present with Him and will have the privilege of ruling and reigning with Him (See Revelation 20:4).

Hence, there will be believers who will be noticeably different from groups two and three, because this first group will have their new bodies while the others will not. These individuals will not procreate nor will they have in their new state the ability to sin. They will also not die. When the Scripture says they will rule with Messiah, their sphere of rule will be determined by their faithfulness to Yeshua during their lifetime.

The second group, Jewish individuals who came to faith after the Rapture, will be called to fulfill Israel's original calling. This calling was to be a light to the Gentiles. Although the first group will be ruling with Messiah and supervising over the Kingdom activity, it is this second group who will be the leaders. Israel will lead the nations in worshipping Messiah and following the laws of G-d. Be assured that in later chapters of this book, a fuller discussion of the activities of the Millennial Kingdom will be presented. In this section, the primary purpose is simply to identify who will be present in this Kingdom. Whereas the first group cannot procreate, those Jewish individuals who come to faith after the Rapture can produce offspring. They can also sin and will die, albeit at a very old age.

The third and final group is that from the nations (Gentiles) who likewise come to faith in Yeshua after the Rapture. They are called to submit to Israel's leadership and adopt a lifestyle that reflects the righteousness of the Torah. They too will be able to procreate. Likewise, sin is a possibility for them and they also will experience death at a very old age.

Once again, all who are present in the Millennial Kingdom

on the first day are believers. However, because two of the three groups can procreate, a fourth group will emerge in the Kingdom. These are the offspring of groups two and three. They will have been born into a new reality. This reality is living under the laws of G-d which are enforced by Messiah Yeshua. This fourth group will know no reality other than the righteous rule of Messiah. They too will be able to procreate, sin, and likewise will live to a very old age. This fourth group and their descendants will eventually make up the largest portion of the inhabitants of the Millennial Kingdom.

It has already been discussed that the reason for the name "Millennial Kingdom" is that this Kingdom will last for one thousand years. Postmillennialists understand the duration of the Kingdom in symbolic terms, because nearly two thousand years have elapsed since Yeshua's ascension from the Mount Olives and return into the heavens. There is a significant reason why this Kingdom will indeed last a thousand years. The number one thousand is a multiple of ten. Numbers such as ten, one hundred, and one thousand, express in Hebrew numerology the concept of "completeness" or "entirety".

The message here is that the Millennial Kingdom will express the purposes of G-d completely or in their entirety. That is, those who will be present during the Millennium will witness firsthand the undeniable manner in which the righteous will of G-d will be maintained. One will not have to be convinced of the reality of HaShem's Messiah, for He will be ruling in their midst. Before discussing the ruling principle for the Millennial Kingdom, and how all inhabitants will be required to live according to it, an overview of Messiah's teaching concerning the Kingdom will be presented.

The Foundation of Messiah's Teaching

The primary issue in this chapter is who will be the inhabitants of the Millennial Kingdom. It has already been shown that on the first day of the Kingdom, all residents will be believers in Messiah. In other words, these are the individuals who have responded correctly to Messiah's teaching of the Gospel. It cannot be over emphasized that the primary message of Yeshua was indeed about the Kingdom. The first statement He made when beginning His formal ministry was, *"Repent, for the Kingdom of heaven is near"* (Matthew 4:17). It is most clear that the focus of Yeshua's teaching was proclaiming how people could be assured that they would be a part of this Kingdom. Although it was clear that repentance was foundational, several of Yeshua's parables were dedicated to describing this Kingdom in a more specific manner and emphasizing certain characteristics of the Kingdom. Three of these parables appear in Matthew chapter 13.

The first of these parables likens the Kingdom to a treasure which is hidden in a field (See Matthew 13:44). When one finds this treasure, he responds in a most curious manner. The text says that he hides it once more and sells all that he has in order to purchase the field. An interesting and significant detail in this parable is that the person who sells all that he owns in order to acquire the treasure, does so with great joy. Most people have to work very hard to acquire all of their life's possessions and, clearly, it would take something very special and of great value to cause them to sell all which they have acquired. Even if the price which he was to receive was of similar worth, it still would be difficult for a person to part with those things that his life represents.

In regard to this concept, I have an example which illustrates this difficulty. A friend of my family bought a piece of land many years ago. It was on this land that he built his family estate. He not only labored hard for many years to complete the project, but he spent a large sum of money to achieve his dream. Nearly thirty years later, when his health was failing him, he decided to sell his estate. Although the price he received was far more than he originally suggested to the real estate agent, when it came time to sign the papers and complete the transaction he was extremely sad to part with the homestead that he felt represented his life and had so many memories attached to it. It is safe to say that although the sale brought him far more money than he ever felt he would possess, "great joy" would not be a phrase that would be used to describe how he felt on that day. As he was driven to the bank to deposit this large sum of money, he displayed remorse.

This is in stark contrast to what one reads in Yeshua's parable concerning the man who had sold all that he possessed and then purchased the field which contained the treasure. It is important for the reader to understand that the joy which is emphasized in this parable did not stem from him utilizing the treasure in some way; rather it was only the fact that he possessed the treasure. It is highly significant that one is never told anything about the nature of this treasure. The only thing which the reader is told is how willing this one who had found the treasure was to part with all that he had, in order to acquire a right to it, and the great joy that such an action caused him. These things did indeed represent a noticeable change in this one's life. It could be said that the things which previously meant a great deal to him and had an important place in his life, were immediately placed aside for what the treasure represented.

In the second parable in this section, the reader encounters an account which, at first glance, is quite similar to the previous one. However, there is one important difference. In this parable (See Matthew 13:45-46) the primary character is not just any man, but one who is a merchant. The text states that this merchant was seeking fine pearls. The point here is that the merchant knows exactly what he wants and he is not sitting, idle, but is pursuing his objective. Although these three parables are three distinct parables, it is important for the reader to understand that they work together to reveal a more complete message. In the first parable the man simply stumbles onto the treasure; but in this second parable, the merchant is well acquainted with that for which he is looking.

The idea that is being expressed in the first parable is that, perhaps, one does not even know of the existence of the Kingdom, but once he learns of it, he should respond in a very dramatic manner. In the second parable, the merchant represents one who knows of the Kingdom's existence and therefore he seeks it. The nuance here is that Messiah is admonishing people of the necessity to seek the Kingdom in a very cognitive and active manner. It is not enough to simply know there is a Kingdom, but one should pursue it and discern its characteristics.

Pearls can vary a great deal and these differences can affect, in a most significant way, the value of each pearl. A pearl merchant must understand these variances and **become aware of the characteristics that give an individual pearl its value.** In a similar manner, it is incumbent upon each individual to learn the qualities of the Kingdom of G-d. Although a single pearl can have a relatively high price, it is highly unlikely that a single pearl could be worth all the assets that one possessed. This is the message that is being highlighted in this second parable; namely that most people undervalue the worth and the significance of the Kingdom, and sadly, would not give all that they have to obtain it. This leads us to the third and final parable in this section.

In this parable, the Kingdom of heaven is likened to a net which is cast into the sea. This net is filled with all kinds of things. Once filled, the net is brought to the shore and that which is in the net is sorted. The good things are obviously separated from the bad. This action requires discernment and a set of standards. Two things are being taught by this parable. The first is that it is not enough to know about the Kingdom and its characteristics, but action is also required. Whereas in the first parable the reader is told that he must sell all that he has in order to acquire the Kingdom, here it requires not just locating the Kingdom, but taking hold of it. The fact that this is likened to casting a net into the sea is most significant. When casting a net into the sea many things are caught in the net and most of these things are not what the one casting the net is seeking. The point is this, when one pursues the Kingdom, the enemy will offer many other things which are counterfeits to the Kingdom. An important aspect of the third parable is that the subject is in the third person plural. Hence, there is a significant change. In the first two parables, the subject relates to the individual, that is, you and me, i.e. humanity. However, because in this third parable the subject is plural, it relates to another entity. Who is this entity? Verses 49-52 answer this question.

Please note that it is only this third parable which contains a summary that provides additional information in order to help the reader interpret the parable properly. Verse 49 reveals the reason why the subject is in the plural. The change in number is to show a change in the subject of the parable, from humanity to the angels. Also in this verse the reader is told the timing for the establishment of the Kingdom, "*the end of the world.*" This fact is extremely problematic for the Postmillennialists who believe that the Kingdom is now, that is, in this age. Putting aside that issue, it is most informative that such a phase as "*the end of the world*" appears.

Judaism asserts that the world (this age) will come to an end by means of G-d's judgment. This is exactly what Messiah Yeshua describes when stating that the angels will go forth and separate the evil ones from the righteous ones. Hence, whereas in the first two parables it is humanity who is exercising discernment, in the third parable it is actually the angels (HaShem's representatives) who are making the choice. What is being relayed to the reader in this verse? It is not so much that humanity chooses the Kingdom, but the Kingdom chooses **some** from humanity. Yeshua is teaching that man must understand and come to the recognition that there is the Kingdom and respond to it. He must pursue it and in doing so must come to an understanding of the "Kingdom Character."

If he rightly learns these things, which are related to the Kingdom, they will have such an impact on this individual that he will be transformed by the Kingdom reality and will be chosen by G-d.

The message of these parables is **NOT** how one is saved. One is saved by grace, apart from any works. It is the sufficiency of Messiah's death on the cross as the payment for sin, and man receiving this by faith, which justifies the believer before G-d. This truth is clearly established by Scripture. If the concluding verses of this section are not dealing with salvation, then just what issue is being addressed? The answer is the outcome of a salvation experience upon the believer. When one finds the Kingdom and responds to it appropriately, he will be moved by it and significant changes will occur. It is important to note that this one is not moved by some inanimate object, for there is a very personal aspect to the Kingdom. The Kingdom would not exist without the King. Central and primary to the Millennial Kingdom is King Messiah. It is when one knows Yeshua and enters into a personal relationship with Him through faith in His grace, i.e. His work of redemption upon the cross, that then the Holy Spirit will dwell in that individual and it is He (Holy Spirit) Who will bring about dramatic changes in this person's life. Although these changes will be numerous, one of their outcomes will be to allow the angels to discern who has responded to the Kingdom reality and who has not. It is this response to the work of Messiah, i.e. the cross, which determines how one is viewed by G-d and His angels.

The text uses the term "the wicked" to describe those who failed to respond to the Kingdom and the term "the just" or "the righteous" in regard to those who have taken upon themselves the Kingdom characteristics by means of their response to the Gospel. This passage is not implying that a person is saved by one's deeds or character, only that when one has truly exercised faith, then he will indeed express a Kingdom character and good works will indeed accompany his redemptive experience. In the next verse (verse 50) "the wicked" are cast into a fiery furnace. Not only does this verse express a judgment, but also poses a problem for one of the tenets of Postmillennialism. As has been previously mentioned, Postmillennialists assert that the preaching of the Gospel will be so successful that the world will be converted by it and Yeshua's return will take place only after a millennium that will end with righteousness, justice, and peace being established for the entire world. Such a view certainly cannot be supported by this parable. This section concludes with an additional statement from Yeshua which could be considered as the fourth parable of this passage. It is because the disciples remarked in verse 51 that they understood what He was teaching, that Yeshua continued and said:

> "...on account of this, every scribe having been instructed in the Kingdom of heaven is like a master of a house who brings forth from his treasure—new and old."
>
> Matthew 13:52

It is no accident that Yeshua spoke concerning a scribe. When the term "scribe" appears in the New Testament, it is not referring to those individuals who merely copied religious texts, as usually is assumed. Rather, it is a reference to those who mandated how the texts were to be copied. Biblical scrolls are copied in a manner which allows the reader to know that at certain locations in the scroll, there were interpretations that needed to be shared with those who were listening. These interpretations also helped them to understand the implications of the text. Spaces between words, sizes of letters, forms of letters, etc. all provided clues to the reader. When the term "the reader" is used, it is a reference to those who would have read the Scriptures before the congregation and also who would have provided a commentary to the listeners. A good example of this occurs in Nehemiah chapter 8:

"And they read in the scroll, in the Law (Torah) of G-d interpreting and placing understanding and granting comprehension in the reading."

Nehemiah 8:8

"The scribes" were not only experts in interpreting the Scriptures, they were actually a political sect within Judaism towards the end of the Second Temple period. Whereas the Pharisees, for example, focused on Jewish law and how one was to implement the commandments into one's life, the scribes, on the other hand, concentrated on the message of the Bible, especially prophecy. Hence, of all the sects in Judaism during the time of Yeshua, it would have been the scribes who would have understood best the Biblical message concerning the Kingdom.

Notice that Yeshua concludes this section by speaking about a scribe who was learned in the Kingdom of heaven. Yeshua likens such a scribe to a head of a house who would bring out his treasured things, both the new and old. What is the significance of such a statement? Bringing out one's possessions, both new and old, relates to one taking an inventory. This inventory would not only consist of a list of what he had, but also the value of these possessions. This inventory, and the value placed on each of these treasured things, would express a great deal concerning that individual. In other words, how one spends his or her money and what possessions one holds onto reveals what is important to that person. The point which Yeshua is teaching is that one who is learned in a proper understanding of the Kingdom will indeed evaluate his or her life in light of the Kingdom and respond in such a way that his life will reflect the righteousness and holiness of this Kingdom. Such an evaluation is not a onetime event, but is frequently repeated throughout one's life.

A similar message is also taught in the parable of the king who had arranged a wedding for his son (See Matthew chapter 22). In this parable, the people clearly knew of the wedding and that it was the king who had prepared the royal banquet (the major part of the wedding). Nevertheless, verse 3 states that they did not want to participate in the wedding of the King's son. In fact, something was more important to them. The parable reveals that they preferred to engage in business activity rather than to participate in the celebration of the king's son and share in the great joy of the king. It is quite significant that some of those who were invited to the wedding even killed the king's servants who bid them to come. What does this piece of information reveal about those individuals?

When a father married off his son or daughter, it was understood in the Biblical culture, to be a great source of joy for that father. Rather than simply rejecting the invitation, the fact that there were some people who responded to the invitation by killing those servants who were bidding people to come, shows that they wanted to stop others from hearing the invitation and therefore prohibiting them from being able to attend. This fact provides evidence that these people were not indifferent to the invitation, but extremely hostile to it. What does the fact that Yeshua included this piece of information in the parable reveal?

People are not indifferent to the Kingdom of G-d or to its message and standards. All people will respond passionately to it in one way or another. Just because all the people did not rise up against the servants and kill them, does not mean that there were some who were indifferent. People can pour their lives into a variety of pursuits, avoiding the Kingdom. Whether they realize it or not, they are demonstrating their opposition to it. Likewise, when one holds opinions, views, and beliefs which are in conflict with the truths of the Kingdom, this also shows hostility to it. For example, at the time of this writing, there is a large push, fueled by recent decisions from the United States Supreme Court, to legitimize same sex marriage in America and embrace the acceptability of homosexuality in general. Those who are in favor of such things are in fact strongly against the Kingdom.

Secularists may want to understand this issue and other moral matters apart from any spiritual connection, but simply denying the spiritual implications does not eliminate them. Sometimes the spiritual realities are clearly manifested. As the Texas House of Legislation (in the summer of 2013) discussed laws that would restrict abortions, those who were protesting against the implementation of any such restrictions were heard singing "Hail Satan." The choice of this "song" speaks volumes concerning these individuals and their relationship to the standards of the Kingdom of G-d. It is unlikely that most of these people would consider themselves to be fighting against the Kingdom. In fact, most would probably not only deny the existence of any future Kingdom of G-d, but also G-d as well; nevertheless these individuals are highly passionate against the Kingdom.

In verse 7, it is clear that the king was angry with those individuals who had murdered his servants and therefore he responded to them by killing them and burning down their city with fire. Certainly this is an image of future judgment and wrath. Again, it is necessary to remember that this parable teaches about the Kingdom and what is revealed by this parable is indeed in conflict with the Postmillennialists' view of the end of this age. The parable concludes with additional servants of the king going out and calling both the bad and the good to the wedding banquet (verse 10). The point here is that one's invitation to the wedding feast, i.e. into the Kingdom, did not depend upon the performance of good deeds nor was it based on any other prerequisites; all were invited. When the king entered and saw his guests and beheld one in attendance who had not dressed in the garments appropriate for a wedding, the king inquired how he had entered into the banquet hall. This one did not have any explanation and was bound and cast outside into darkness where there is weeping and gnashing of teeth (See verses 11-13).

Obviously, a person is not going to be allowed to enter

into the Kingdom by mistake, so what is the message of this portion of the parable? The invitation to the wedding, i.e. into the Kingdom, did not bring about any change in this person. Why not? The answer is that this one had not truly responded properly to the message of the Kingdom. The fact that he lacked any evidence that he had truly received the Gospel represents a situation that is impossible. The New Testament is clear, if one is in Messiah, he is a new creation and behold all things are new (See 2 Corinthians 5:17). This change comes about because of the indwelling of the Holy Spirit. It is inconceivable that the Holy Spirit enters into to an individual and there not be any noticeable results of this. Hence, Yeshua is simply teaching that a true response to the invitation to enter the Kingdom (Gospel) will bring about evidence of that decision which will be seen in and through this one's life. The fact that this one appears at the wedding banquet in his same clothes, rather than dressed in a manner which is appropriate for the event, i.e. the Kingdom; reveals that this one had never truly received the Gospel and therefore will not be part of the wedding banquet, i.e. the Kingdom.

In the New Testament, Yeshua told more than 30 different parables. It is safe to say that nearly all of them related in some manner to the Kingdom. Although several are presented as revealing what the Kingdom is like, the vast majority of them contain an emphasis on how to enter into the Kingdom (salvation) or the proper motivation that one should possess for entering the Kingdom. It is most interesting that the parables which do indeed relate to what the Kingdom is like, provide very little detailed information about it. It is similar to a real estate agent telling a person how terrific a home is, and that everyone would want to own it, and the various things people are doing to raise the funds to purchase this home, but never telling any of the particular details of the home, or being willing to show this home to any of his clients. In other words, one would have to rely on the claims of the realtor alone. Perhaps if one really trusted this particular realtor, and was convinced that he knew exactly what the client wanted, he would put in an offer on the house without ever seeing it.

This is the point which such parables want to teach the reader concerning the Kingdom. Yeshua never tells the precise details of what the Kingdom will be, although He provides a few examples. The reader must respond based on the fact that it is Yeshua Who is making the invitation and, of course, the fact of what He was willing to do to make the Kingdom a possibility for humanity, i.e. the cross. This alone should provide the basis for one responding faithfully to His Kingdom invitation.

The Cross and the Kingdom

In the tenth chapter of Matthew, Yeshua offers some of His most poignant teachings concerning the Kingdom. It is very significant that the previous chapter ended with a reference to the harvest. The harvest in this context clearly refers to the gathering up of those who will be in the Kingdom. The final verse in this chapter (Matthew 9:38) admonishes the hearer to pray. The reason for this prayer is because, although there is a great potential for a large harvest, there is a need for laborers to do the work of the harvest.

Before surveying the tenth chapter of Matthew, it is important for one to remember that the term harvest conveys a time of celebration with great joy. It is a time when expectations and hopes are to be realized. The farmer planted in faith, and prayed for a harvest that would be many fold his initial investment. The primary question that chapter ten addresses is: what are the necessary steps that Yeshua's disciples must take in order to bring about a great Kingdom harvest? Once again, this is not the focus of this book, but the message of this chapter reveals the importance of Israel and the role that Israel will have in establishing the Kingdom.

The chapter opens with Yeshua calling His twelve disciples

and giving them authority over unclean spirits and all types of sickness and disease. Perhaps the first question that should be asked is: why twelve disciples? Obviously, the number twelve relates to the twelve tribes of Israel. Is Yeshua replacing them with twelve other individuals, demonstrating G-d's dissatisfaction and rejection of Israel? Although there are theologians who assert such a position, as the reader will learn later in this chapter, context and content prohibit such an interpretation. Furthermore, in the book of Revelation, John speaks about the 24 elders, referring to both the twelve tribes and the twelve disciples. When he speaks about the twelve gates of the New Jerusalem, he also unites them with the twelve tribes of Israel. It is important for the reader to understand that in Hebrew numerology, the number twelve relates to the people of G-d. Therefore, in Matthew chapter ten, the twelve disciples relate to a future reality when it will be the people of G-d who will be given authority over unclean spirits and all types of sickness and disease and will use this authority to establish the Kingdom. In other words, chapter ten foreshadows, not only the establishment of the Kingdom, but an important aspect of the Kingdom—namely, it will be devoid of unclean spirits and disease.

Concerning these twelve disciples, Yeshua commands them **not** to go in the way of the Gentiles or into any city of the Samaritans; rather **only** to the lost sheep of the house of Israel. It is precisely to Israel that the Kingdom is preached! Why is this? The answer is to emphasize the relationship between the Kingdom and Israel. This truth ought not be ignored or rejected. It is an absolute requirement that Israel, i.e. the Jewish people, come to faith in Messiah in order for the Kingdom to be established. This is why Yeshua said:

> "For I say unto you, 'You shall not see Me henceforth, until you shall say, Blessed is the One Who comes in the Name of the L-RD'".
>
> Matthew 23:39

When it is said that the Jewish people must come to faith in Yeshua prior to the establishment of the Kingdom on earth, it is important for one to understand the implications of this statement. This statement does not speak concerning the Jewish people throughout the ages, for once one dies, Jew or Gentile, his opportunity to accept Messiah and be redeemed has passed. This statement relates only to those Jewish individuals who are alive at the end of this age. As the Prophets declared, not only will the Jewish people return to their historic homeland, but a great number of them will turn to Messiah Yeshua during, and especially at the end of, the period of time known as "Jacob's trouble," a time of intense persecution of the Jewish people at the end of this age.

In essence, chapter ten is demonstrating one key aspect of what will take place in the last days. Therefore, the twelve disciples are being commanded to do the very thing that Yeshua's disciples should be doing and, G-d willing, will be doing at the end of this age. As will be shown later on, this tenth chapter is very eschatological (dealing with the last days) in nature. Not only does Yeshua instruct them to preach the Kingdom, but in the very same statement He continues and commands them:

> "*Sick ones heal, lepers cleanse, dead ones raise, demons cast out.*"
>
> Matthew 10:8

Such activities are also found in Biblical prophecy and in rabbinical literature. These sources as well relate these activities to the Messianic era. Those who fail to heed these signs and to respond appropriately to the proclamation of Yeshua's followers, will suffer a harsh judgment. For Yeshua warns:

> "*Truly I say to you, it shall be more tolerable for the land of Sodom and Gomorrah in judgment day than for that city.*"
>
> Matthew 10:15

During the time prior to Yeshua's ascension, the twelve disciples did not meet the type of opposition that verses 16-23 speak of.

"Behold, I am sending you as sheep in the midst wolves; therefore you be wise as the serpents and innocent as the doves. But take heed of man, for they will deliver you to the councils and into their assemblies they will flog you. And unto rulers and even kings you will be brought on account of Me for a witness to them and to the nations (Gentiles). And whatever is given to you, give no thought on what to speak, for it will be given in that hour what you should say. For it is not you who are the speakers, but the Spirit of your Father is the One speaking in you. And brother will deliver brother to death and father children, and children will rise up against parent and put them to death. And you will be hated by all on account of My name, but the one who endures until the end will be saved. And whenever they persecute you in that city, flee into another, for truly I say unto you by no means will you exhaust all the cities of Israel until the Son of Man will come."

Matthew 10:16-23

Although the Apostles did endure persecution and believers suffered great persecution during the latter period of the Roman Empire, it is clear that Yeshua is referring in this section to the end of this age. This view is easily supported when one considers that many of the verses are nearly identical to the Olivet Discourse in Mark chapter 13:

"But look out for yourselves, for you shall be delivered into councils and in synagogues you shall be scourged, and unto rulers and kings you shall be for My sake, for a testimony to them. And into all the nations it is necessary first to proclaim the Gospel. But when they lead you and

*deliver you, do not be anxious before on what to say, nor be
concerned. For whatever shall be given to you in that hour,
this speak, for it not you who will be speaking, rather the
Holy Spirit. And brother will deliver brother to death and
father a child, and children will rise up against parent and
they will put them to death; and you will be hated by all on
account of My name. But the one who perseveres unto the
end, this one will be saved."*

Mark 13:9, 11-13

*"But whenever they shall persecute you in that city, flee
into another; for truly I say to you 'you should by no means
exhaust all the cities of Israel, until the Son of Man will
come."*

Matthew 10:23

There can be no doubt that prior to Messiah's Second
Coming, there must be an emphasis on not simply Jewish
evangelism, but also on reaching those Jewish individuals
dwelling in Israel. Once again, the primary focus of this book is
not on the events of the last days, but rather on the Millennial
Kingdom, which will be established at the end of the last days.
Therefore, what will be stressed when dealing with the second
half of this chapter is not the events, but the state of mind of
those with whom Messiah will be well pleased.

A Kingdom Mindset

It is possible to summarize the second half of Matthew ten
with one word: humility. It is a Biblically based humility that
will cause one to submit to the will of G-d and endure intense
persecution because of one's faith in Messiah Yeshua. Persecution
for followers of Messiah Yeshua is a foreign concept for much
of Western civilization today. Christianity has dominated most

of the West during the last several hundred years. The United States of America was founded on a religious freedom that guaranteed not only Christians, but all individuals, the right to practice their religious beliefs without the fear of persecution. Such freedom did not come without a high cost. One cannot over emphasize the number of martyrs who gave their lives and secured the freedom that not only Christians, but those of other religious faiths, enjoy in the West.

It is clear from Matthew ten that these freedoms are going to gradually be lost in the last days and those who embrace Messiah Yeshua will be hated, persecuted and some will even be put to death. Such persecution is increasingly common in many parts of the world; in fact, in many Muslim countries, being a believer in Yeshua is a death sentence. What would cause one to behave in such a way, that they would be a recipient of such hatred and persecution? The answer is submission to the teachings of Yeshua. Humility plays a large role in such submissiveness because one must reach the conclusion that the message which Yeshua taught, and faithfulness to Him, is more important than one's individual life.

It is clear that in the last days there will be a great corruption of society as immorality will be embraced as proper and even praiseworthy conduct. A good example of this is when the President of the United States announced in 2012 that he supports same sex marriage. His proclamation was responded to with applause and media outlets lauded him for taking a "brave" stance. It is those who view such a position as ungodly and homosexuality as an abomination, who are ridiculed and seen as "hateful" people. Slowly but clearly, those who state the Biblical position on such immorality are beginning to experience non-violent forms of persecution, but in time physical responses are sure to come.

Yeshua, in this section of chapter ten, commands His followers to speak out the revelation that is received from Him:

*"Therefore do not fear them, for there is nothing which
has been concealed which will not be revealed and hidden
which will not be known. The thing I say to you in darkness,
you speak in the light and the thing in the ear you hear, you
proclaim on the rooftops."*

Matthew 10:26-27

Once again, the purpose of relating these things is not to
discuss the events of the last days, but simply to point out the
attitude and the mentality of those who will take a righteous
stance in the end times. These individuals will indeed face
much persecution. Although it has already been stated that
a submissive and humble mindset will cause an individual
to behave properly during such affliction, one must ask the
question: what brings about in the believer, this type of mindset?
The answer is love. Not a natural love that one may feel for a
spouse or family members, but a love that is heavenly in nature.
This love is one of the fruits of the Spirit (See Galatians 5:22).
It is important to note that only followers of Messiah have the
potential to display this love. This means not every believer is
going to possess it because such love is an outcome of spiritual
growth and maturity. An illustration of this love appears in the
Song of Songs. King Solomon writes:

"...for as strong as death is love..."

Songs of Songs 8:6

This verse reveals that there is an inherent connection
between love and death. It is possible to even say that a godly
love brings about death. Jewish sages understand this and relate
the death spoken of in this verse to a change which takes place
first and foremost in the individual. These sages understand
that this heavenly love brings about the death of what Judaism
calls the רצי ערה (evil inclination) This inclination brings about
in humanity what is best understood as "selfishness". Each

person, because he or she is a descendant of Adam, has this inclination.

However, when the believer receives the Gospel and is immediately filled with the Holy Spirit, he becomes a new creation and therefore is given the potential to overcome this inclination and love HaShem, rather than self. Yeshua revealed an important relationship between the love of G-d and the ability to love others instead of self, when He united two commandments from the Torah. When He was asked what is the greatest of the commandments, He answered, "To love the L-rd your G-d with all your heart, soul, mind, and strength." The interesting nuance that Yeshua brought out is how He continued and remarked that the second (to the greatest commandment) is **like it** and quoted from Leviticus 19 and said, "You shall love your neighbor as yourself."

The issue that must be explored is why Yeshua said that loving the L-rd your G-d is **like** loving your neighbor as yourself. Most scholars understand Yeshua's intent for making this statement is to reveal that it is only when an individual is in a covenantal relationship with HaShem that this one is able to love his neighbor properly. In other words, experiencing the love of G-d is foundational for changing one's love of self into a godly love for others.

Once again it is this type of love for another which will characterize the Millennial Kingdom. Such a love is most foreign to those who are not in covenant with G-d by means of faith in Messiah Yeshua. Those individuals will, in the last days, actually turn against members of their own family in order to avoid the persecution of governments who will want to arrest, imprison, torture, and kill followers of Yeshua.

The tenth chapter of Matthew concludes with a section that has the word "reward" appearing three times. There is no doubt that there is a connection between the concept of reward and the Kingdom. Love is once again emphasized and the reader is told that if one's love for Yeshua is not greater than even the love this person has for family, then he is not worthy of Yeshua. Denying oneself and enduring much suffering is the outcome of following Yeshua and such behavior is related in this section by the verse:

> *"And the one who does not take up his cross and follow after Me is not worthy of Me."*
>
> Matthew 10:38

The point which must be stressed is that there is an important connection between the cross and the Kingdom. Usually one thinks of the term "the cross" as only relating to Yeshua's death and the payment His death made to ensure that believers would receive the forgiveness of sin and thereby be able to enter into the Kingdom. However, what is being stressed by Yeshua in this section, in addition to what has already been said, is that the same attitude that led Yeshua to lay down His life on the cross, will also be the attitude that His disciples will possess and demonstrate in word and deed. What will be a surprise to many believers is that the Torah and the cross have an interesting relationship between them. It is this relationship that will be the focus of the next chapter.

Chapter 2

THE TORAH AND THE KINGDOM

One cannot overemphasize the significance of Isaiah's words when he states:

> "And it will come about in the last days, the mountain of the L-rd's house (Temple) will be established at the head of the mountains and it will be exalted above the hills and all the nations will stream unto it. And many people will walk and they will say, 'Let us go up to the mountain of the L-rd, to the house of the G-d of Jacob and He will teach us His ways and we will walk in His paths'. **For from Zion will go forth the Torah and the word of the L-rd from Jerusalem."**
>
> Isaiah 2:2-4

Although there are many implications to the words of Isaiah, the primary point that I want to make first is that the Law of Moses still has relevance and will be the standard on which Messiah will base His rule during the Millennial Kingdom. For many within the Church, such a statement goes against what they have been taught. One of the most crippling tendencies among a large portion of Christians today is a failure to study prophecy.

This failure will leave the Church unprepared for what will occur in the end times and is the root cause for a growing percentage of Christians to reject the existence of the Millennial Kingdom and to fail to understand the significant role that Israel, both the land and the people, will play in the last days and in the Millennial Kingdom. If one has been taught that there is no more relevance to the Torah then what is one to do with a future era which will be governed according to the Torah? As previously stated, the answer for some is to simply deny that there is a Millennial Kingdom.

Before progressing further in the discussion of a Torah based Kingdom, it is necessary to answer why the Torah will be used by G-d in the future and what would have caused the vast majority of Christians to have missed this point. The answer in regard to the latter question is, in short, an improper understanding of Paul's teaching concerning the Law. Paul clearly placed Law and faith (faith in the grace offered by Messiah Yeshua) as two elements that in some ways were at odds with one another. This tendency most commonly appears when the subject being discussed was justification. Paul on several occasions stated:

> "*But knowing that a man is not justified out of works of Torah (Law); rather by means of faith of Messiah Yeshua...*"
> Galatians 2:16

It is important to make a distinction between what Scripture actually states and what was a commonly held belief which Israel's leaders taught at the end of the Second Temple period. Although one does not find within the Hebrew Bible (Old Testament) any basis for believing that G-d provided the Law of Moses as an instrument that justifies or saves an individual, late Second Temple period Judaism clearly asserted this view.

Hence, Paul's frequent disparaging words concerning the Law was not in regard to HaShem's purpose for providing it, rather it was aimed at the rabbinical distortion regarding the purpose of the Torah. Paul made numerous positive statements concerning the Law. For example:

> *"Therefore, the Torah is holy and the commandment is holy and righteous and good."*
>
> Romans 7:12

> *"Therefore what shall we say, the Law is sin? G-d forbid! Rather, I would have not known sin, except by means of the Law..."*
>
> Romans 7:7

In these verses Paul restates one of the Scriptural purposes for the Law, namely to assist man in knowing what is sin. Theologians also have correctly linked the Torah to righteousness, but only in the sense that in a similar way that one recognizes what is sin by means of the Law, he can now recognize what is righteous through the Torah.

In turning now to the former issue of why the Torah would be the basis for Yeshua's rule during the Millennial Kingdom, it is important to remember how righteousness is linked to the Torah. Again, it is not that Torah observance is the means to righteousness (or justification), but simply that the Torah defines what is righteousness.

In speaking about the Kingdom, Yeshua said these words:

> *"But seek first the Kingdom of G-d and His righteousness..."*
>
> Matthew 6:33

It is clear that Yeshua links the Kingdom to the concept of righteousness. Since righteousness is defined by the Torah, and Isaiah speaks of the Torah going forth from Zion, i.e. the Millennial Kingdom, it does not require any leap of faith to arrive at the conclusion that Yeshua will rule from Jerusalem according to the Torah. In other words, it is because Yeshua will enforce Torah law that righteousness will be maintained in the Kingdom. In returning to the verse from Matthew's Gospel, it is interesting to note how the verse concludes:

> "*But seek first the Kingdom of G-d and His righteousness,*
> ***and all these things will be added unto you.***"
> Matthew 6:33

What are the implications of the phrase "***and all these things will be added unto you***?" The idea here is that when one pursues righteousness, G-d will, in turn, respond and be active in this person's life in order to bless him with the various material and spiritual needs that each person has. This verse actually concludes a greater discussion about the cares of life. Within the Greek text (Matthew 6:33) the word δὲ appears. Although this word is ignored by many of the English translations, it has great significance. This word is a conjunction which unites the previous thought or thoughts with what is being said in the current verse. The important point here is that although the word δὲ unites these two thoughts, the primary purpose of this word is to show a contrast between them. Hence, whereas it was normal for individuals to place a priority on the basic needs of life, what Yeshua is stressing to His followers is that this is not how they should behave. In other words, Yeshua is teaching that in contrast to the worldly view that places a greater priority (first) on the needs of one's life, His disciples are to seek first the Kingdom of G-d and His righteousness and then they can be assured that HaShem will respond to them by blessing them with the material necessities.

One should not fail to notice that the word "*seek*" is in the imperative mood, i.e. in the form of a command! Therefore, it is not an option to seek the Kingdom of G-d and His righteousness, but an absolute requirement for believers. The second half of the command is a type of checks and balances. Many can believe that they are indeed seeking the Kingdom of G-d, but in reality they may not be doing so. The key in determining whether one is, in fact, pursuing the Kingdom of G-d is whether or not His (G-d's) righteousness is being pursued and established. It may be hard for an individual to determine in his own mind whether this criterion is being met. Hence, Torah law provides a qualitative basis for determining this.

The point here is that it is impossible for one to define the Kingdom, apart from HaShem and His righteousness. It is an absolute necessity that the concept of righteousness be defined by Scripture alone and not simply by one's personal view of what he thinks is right and what he thinks is wrong. Many err in simply assuming that they, as a believer, now know inherently what righteousness is. This same error plagues all other religious expressions as well. Obviously as believers in Yeshua and students of the Tanach (Old Testament) and the New Testament, we know that the G-d of our Bible is indeed righteous. However, when one fails to do the necessary study of Scripture so that he can arrive at a Biblically based definition and understanding of righteousness, then this one is at a great disadvantage and will most certainly err in his understanding of righteousness and for that matter what the Kingdom will be like. It is because of this, that many believers lack the framework to interpret whether their lifestyle choices and viewpoints are pleasing to G-d or not. Because of this failure and its high frequency, the behavior of a large portion of Yeshua's followers is most similar to the ways of the world. Failure to understand G-d in a Scripturally-based righteousness will naturally also lead to a failure to be able to discern truth in general. This is why so many followers of Yeshua support political positions which are in clear conflict with Biblical truth.

The following provides a good example of how some fail

to discern truth. Judaism and an ever increasing number of
Christians, understand the Islamic god, Allah, as the one true
G-d, Who was first revealed in the Old Testament and was
finally revealed in the New Testament. In regard to this point,
it is also vital to affirm that it is **ONLY** in these two places that
the One True G-d has been revealed. Judaism incorrectly states
that the G-d of the Old Testament and Allah are in fact the One
and same G-d because it has failed to properly compare the
Scriptural attributes of HaShem to Allah and what the Koran
reveals about him.

If one examines the authoritative texts of both Judaism and
Islam, it becomes quite clear that the attributes and the standards
belonging to HaShem are most different than those which the
Koran associates with Allah and, therefore, HaShem and Allah
cannot be one and the same. In addition to this, the theological
conclusions which are derived from the examination of other
Scriptural matters within the Hebrew Bible and the Koran are
most different.

Even though the Koran borrows several accounts from the
Hebrew Bible and the Christian Bible, the use of them clearly
shows that the values, judgments, and affirmations that Islam
holds are not the same as the Judeo-Christian teachings. Islam's
view of Yeshua is certainly not in line with that of the New
Testament. For example the Koran states:

> "*Jesus (Yeshua) said: 'I am indeed a slave of Allah, Allah is
> my lord and your lord, so worship him alone.'*"
>
> Quran 3:51

Because the commandments of a given religion manifest
a great deal about the character and nature of the deity who
gave these commandments, it is most helpful for one who
wishes to understand the righteousness of HaShem, which will
characterize and define the Millennial Kingdom, to examine the
Torah. Problems arise, as previously stated, when righteousness

is not defined by the Law, but left to a person's own subjective views. When a person fails to or rejects to utilize the Torah (the 613 Biblical commandments which appear in the first five books of the Bible) as the main source for defining righteousness, then this one must use some other standard for arriving at his definition of righteousness.

What other standard can be used? There is a growing tendency among a segment of Christianity which states that it is the character of Messiah Yeshua that defines the righteousness of the Kingdom and not the Torah. There is no problem with such a perspective, except the failure of these Christians to understand that the character which Yeshua expresses is indeed the same righteousness which the Torah expresses. The fact that these Christians see differences between the righteousness of Messiah Yeshua and that of the Torah demonstrates a serious flaw with their understanding of Yeshua in general.

Their error is usually based in an oversimplification of Yeshua. It is clear that in the four Gospels, Yeshua is presented as righteous. No believer would argue this point; however, what must be understood by believers is how the Gospels convey this point. When Luke, for example, begins his account, he starts with the parents of John the Baptist, Zacharias and Elizabeth. The first thing that is said concerning them is:

"*And they were both righteous before G-d going in all the commandments and righteous standards of the L-rd (they were) blameless.*"

Luke 1:6

It is significant that the phrase "*righteous standards*", which is frequently translated in most English translations simply as "ordinances", is the Greek word δικαιώμασιν. It is formed from the same Greek word that appears earlier in the verse stating that both Zacharias and Elizabeth were righteous.

The point here is that the New Testament chose a word which

emphasizes the righteousness of the Law and one's obedience to it as the basis for one being presented and understood as righteous. (Please note, in no way is the text stating that Zacharias and Elizabeth were in some way without sin and not in need of justification or that one is justified by the observance of the Law.) Rather, it means that these two individuals applied the Law to their lives as the divine standard for one's behavior. One must remember that much of the Torah deals with how to properly respond with one's sin.

The verse from Luke could also be understood to mean, and I would argue should be understood as, not speaking about two separate things, commandments and righteous standards, but rather the use of the Greek word καὶis is being used emphatically, in order to modify or describe the commandments. The phrase could be translated:

> "*And they were both righteous before G-d going in all the commandments **even** the righteousness of the L-rd (they were) blameless.*"
>
> Luke 1:6

In other words, Luke is conveying to the reader that the commandments of G-d are not just HaShem's righteous regulations, but they can and should be understood as defining the righteousness of G-d.

Likewise Joseph, the legal father of Yeshua, is described in a very significant manner:

> "*And Joseph her husband, being righteous...*"
>
> Matthew 1:19

The Greek word used here to describe Joseph is the same word that appears in Luke 1:6. Most English translations prefer to render it in this verse as "just", which is acceptable, as long as one properly understands that Biblically speaking, "justice" and "righteousness" are indeed the same thing (for there are not two different words in the New Testament for these two English concepts).

Another individual who appears early in Luke's account is Simeon (Shimon). He also is quickly connected to Yeshua:

> *"And behold there was a man in Jerusalem whose name (was) Shimon and this man (was) righteous and devout waiting for the comfort of Israel; and the Holy Spirit was upon him. It was revealed to him by the Holy Spirit, he would not see death before he should see HaShem's Messiah. And he came by means of the Spirit into the Temple and when the parents brought the Child Yeshua that they do to Him according to the custom of the Torah concerning Him."*
> Luke 2:25-27

Once again Shimon, like others who are associated with Messiah Yeshua, is described with the word "righteous." Why was it that Shimon's and Yeshua's paths collided? Some would simply answer: because it was promised to Shimon that he would see the Messiah before he died. Although this is true, what needs to be emphasized is how this promise was, in fact, fulfilled. It was only because Yeshua's parents came to Jerusalem in order to perform the requirements of the Law. In Leviticus chapter 12 there are certain requirements that must be done after a child is born. Most people know about the commandment to circumcise, but there is also an additional commandment which comes 33 days after the circumcision. It was because of this commandment which the parents were observing that Shimon met Yeshua. Once again, it was because of the Law and those who applied it to their lives that HaShem's plan was advanced.

In this passage, which deals with Shimon meeting Yeshua, it is very significant that the Messiah is called "The Comfort of Israel;" additional proof that it is Biblically incorrect to hold a view concerning the end times that does not concern Israel and the Jewish people. Some theologians are quick to point out that this event was in regard to Yeshua's first coming and not His second, therefore, they claim it is improper to relate this text with the last days. The problem with such a perspective is that while it is true that this event took place during His first coming, the title "The Comfort of Israel" will not be fulfilled until He returns. Later on in this same section, Yeshua is called a "Light unto the Gentiles" and the "Glory of Your People Israel" (See verse 32). Both of these terms will ultimately be realized only at the end of the age. This is why Shimon said additionally:

> "...*Behold this One is appointed for a falling and a rising of many in Israel and for a sign which is disputed.*"
>
> Luke 2:34

This verse makes it clear that Shimon's prophecy, which he addressed to Miriam (Mary), concerns not just the work of His first coming, but is also in regard to the entire time, from His ascension to His return, and the establishing of His Kingdom. There is also something very important about this time.

Currently we are in the midst of a discussion of how the concept of righteousness surrounds Yeshua's life. We have seen that early on in His life those whom the Scripture placed alongside of Him were described with the word "righteous." Furthermore, when one examines Yeshua's life, it becomes very clear, according to the Scriptures, that He is absolutely righteous. What is another way for this point to be stated? It could be said that Yeshua never violated any of the Torah commandments. In fact, one of the key aspects of the Gospel accounts is that the Pharisees, Chief Priests, and other leaders attempted repeatedly to demonstrate that Yeshua had transgressed the Law.

This point they, of course, could **never** substantiate. This fact, however, emphasizes the inherent relationship between

Yeshua and the Torah. This relationship, although clear in the Scripture, is virtually never acknowledged by Christianity. Rather the common position of the Church is that it is precisely because of the work of Messiah, that the Law is done away with and it does not have any relevance whatsoever today, or for that matter in the future. Perhaps this position is embraced because Yeshua Himself says that He came to fulfill the Law and the Prophets (Matthew 5:17-19). It is this point, when rightly understood, that actually underscores the nature of the Kingdom and its connection to the Torah. We shall explore this further in chapter seven.

At the end of the previous chapter, it was said that this chapter would focus upon the interesting relationship between the Torah and the Cross. Here again, a large percentage of Christians would understand the Torah and the Cross as relating to two different means of obtaining salvation. This, as previously stated, is false! The Torah was never suggested in the Old Testament as a means or a way of obtaining salvation. Rather, the Torah is presented as a standard of conduct which manifests righteousness. Also contained within the Torah are actions that must be taken when one violates a commandment (obviously a reference to the sacrificial system). Yet nowhere in the Old Testament is the Torah ever presented as an instrument of redemption. Quite the contrary, the Torah reveals a person's **need for redemption**, as this is one of Paul's major messages. In his epistle to the Galatians, Paul succinctly states this. First of all he writes:

> *"For if by Torah is the inheritance, it is no longer based in a promise; but to Abraham by means of a promise, G-d having graced."*
>
> Galatians 3:18

This translation sounds a bit odd. What does it mean "*G-d having graced*"? Most other translations simply translate the

verb as "gave grace". The actual word is κεχάρισται and its literal
meaning is "to be gracious" or "to forgive". Hence, Paul reveals
that the promise which HaShem made to Abraham, namely
HaShem's desire to bless all the families of the earth, contained
grace. This grace has many significant outcomes, one of which is
the forgiveness of sin. This being the case, why was there a need
for the Torah? As has been stated repeatedly, the Law defines
righteousness. To this end Paul continues to write:

> *"Therefore what is the Torah? On account of transgression*
> *it was added until the Seed should come of Whom the*
> *promise had been made..."*
>
> Galatians 3:19

This verse is so important in providing the context for
one to understand the intent of the Abrahamic Covenant.
It has already been seen that this covenant contained grace
and forgiveness. However humanity, for the most part, did
not perceive this nor comprehend the need for this grace.
In other words, the world was not sensitive to its sin, i.e. its
unrighteousness. It was because of this insensitivity, that
man would not perceive his need for Messiah, the Seed of
the Abrahamic Covenant. It is for this reason that Paul states
that the Torah was given: in order to make man aware of his
transgression and therefore make him seek the Savior. With
this understanding it is now quite reasonable to comprehend
why Paul would write:

> *"Therefore, is the Torah against the promises of G-d? G-d*
> *forbid, for if the Law had been given that was able to give*
> *life, certainly from the Torah would there be righteousness."*
>
> Galatians 3:21

It is most important for the reader to understand exactly
what Paul is saying and what he is not saying in this verse. First,

he clearly asserts that the Torah does **not** provide life. What does he mean by this? Paul's intent is to clarify that by no means does the Torah provide the way whereby one is able to enter into the Kingdom of G-d. Secondly, the outcome of the Law is **not** righteousness. One must be very careful here. Even though the Torah does not produce righteousness within an individual, it does in fact define what righteousness is and therefore what is unrighteous as well. This point is quite elementary, yet a large segment of Christians stumble over it. Perhaps the following illustration will assist in our discussion.

Recently I had a physical in which a series of tests were performed. When I received the results, not only did I receive my individual "scores," but also the numbers that reflected what was normal. Hence, these base numbers represented what was proper for healthy people, and when my results varied from these base numbers, it revealed a problem with my health.

Although these base numbers served a purpose in manifesting abnormalities in my health, obviously these base numbers played absolutely no role whatsoever in making me healthy. In a like manner, the Torah, when applied to my life, will show areas where I am violating G-d's standards of righteousness, but the Law plays no role in actually bringing about a change in a person or making one righteous. Rather, as Paul states, it was added until the Seed, i.e. Messiah Yeshua should come. It is this fact that Paul returns to in the next verse:

> "But the Scripture confined all under sin, in order that the promise (should come) by faith of Messiah Yeshua, given to the ones who believe."
>
> Galatians 3:22

Once again, by means of the Law, all individuals are manifested to be sinners and therefore in need of grace and forgiveness, which is available to sinners only through the

Seed, i.e. Messiah Yeshua. However, prior to Messiah Yeshua's coming, Paul continues and states:

> "*But before faith came, we were held in custody by the Torah, confined up until that faith could be manifested; with the result that the Law should be our tutor until Messiah, in order that we should be justified by faith.*"
>
> Galatians 3:23-24

It is clear in these verses that the Law and faith in Messiah Yeshua are not mutually exclusive, but work together as two integral parts of HaShem's plan. The problem occurs when one fails to understand the proper implications of the next verse:

> "*But after faith has come, we are no longer under a tutor.*"
>
> Galatians 3:25

This verse has caused most of Christianity to view the tutor, i.e. the Law, as a thing of the past and having no relevance for the believer today; but this is not the intent of the verse at all. Special attention must be given to the phrase, "under a tutor". The intent of the word "under" should be understood as referring to judgment, as one who is "under judgment". In other words, to say that one is no longer under a tutor in this context means that one is no longer under Torah judgment. The simple implication to this is that no longer does the Torah have the authority to condemn the believer.

What this phrase does not mean is that everything the tutor taught is now no longer relevant for the believer. Certainly the wisdom that the tutor taught is still true and practical and one should follow it. Furthermore, there may be times when the young man will want to consult with his tutor after their formal relationship has ended. Returning now to our discussion of the Torah, a believer should understand that the best means of manifesting to man what is righteous, and therefore what is unrighteous, is still the Torah (illuminated by the Holy Spirit).

Perhaps another example would assists in bringing this point home. When I was a child, I had a very strict bedtime. As I became older, I was allowed to stay up later, but nevertheless, a bedtime was still enforced by my father. However, when I became sixteen years old my father took away my bedtime. I could hardly believe it. I responded to him, "You mean I can stay up as late as I want to and there is no punishment?" My father said, "Not exactly." There is a punishment, but it would not be from him. I did not understand and asked, "Then from whom?" He said that the purpose of the bedtime was to teach me that receiving a proper amount of sleep is important and that when one fails to receive enough sleep, he will not function at his best the next day. But now that I was sixteen, I should be mature enough to make that decision of when to go to bed for myself. If I chose to go to sleep at 2:00 a.m. he was not going to punish me, but there was a punishment. Again I asked, "From whom?" The answer was from the violation of the principle itself. When one goes to bed at 2:00 a.m. and gets up at 6:00 a.m. he feels the punishment when the alarm clock goes off and sometimes all day long.

This is the point concerning the Law. When one violates the Torah it can have both physical and spiritual ramifications. Although this is true once again for the believer, it no longer has the power to bring death or to keep him out of the Kingdom. Why not? The answer reveals the important relationship between the Law and the Cross.

When Moses speaks of the Torah, he describes it as containing life and death, blessing and curse (See Deuteronomy 11:26-28 and 30:15, 19). In other words, it defines how a person should live and if one fails to live in that manner, then the result will be death. Similarly, for the obedient one a Torah observant lifestyle brings blessings, while the one who sins finds curses. The problem is that although the Law is holy, just, and good

(See Roman 7:12); placed upon sinful humanity, it always will bring curse and ultimately death. It is for this reason that Paul asks if the Torah, which is good, actually will bring death unto a person (see Romans 7:13).

To this question Paul answers strongly in the negative. He wants to reveal to the reader that it was not the Law that brought death to humanity, rather, sin. The Torah only manifested this sin and, thereby, revealed man's true spiritual condition of being dead before HaShem. Once again, it is only the Torah which has the purpose of showing man his need for repentance. It must be pointed out that true repentance seeks redemption; and from where does redemption originate? If one simply answers from the Messiah, then the answer is not complete. The proper answer is the Messiah and Him crucified. One must remember that Messiah came into this world heading for one location— the Cross!

In the Gospels, Messiah spoke frequently about "*His time*" and that "*His time had not yet come.*" To what was He referring? The correct response is the Cross. Although Paul stated he delights in the Law (Romans 7:22), and acknowledges that it is spiritual, nevertheless, in his current condition he is dead and the Law (Torah) cannot do one thing to alter this condition. What is this current condition? Paul states in Romans 7:14 that he is "*carnal and sold under sin.*" What does the phrase "*sold under sin*" mean? Once again, the idea here is similar to what was stated concerning the phrase "under the tutor." Paul is under the judgment or condemnation that sin brings. It is for this reason that he cries out:

> "*I am a miserable man, who will save me from this body of death?*"
>
> Romans 7:24

The answer is, of course, Messiah Yeshua, but how does Yeshua save one from his miserable condition? The answer is of course the Cross!

Why the Cross?

Most Jewish individuals would assert that the cross has absolutely nothing to do with Judaism. However, they would readily accept the Torah as being the very foundation upon which Judaism is based. This perspective is highly flawed. In actuality, the Law and the Cross are inherently related to one another. It was only because of the Law that the Cross has significance. Without the Cross, Messiah would not have fulfilled His work of redemption for which the Torah manifested the need. It was not that Yeshua simply had to die; rather He had to die specifically upon the Cross. Recently I asked a student of mine, why was it that the Messiah had to die on the Cross? His answer was because it was the most tortuous manner of death at that time. Yes, Messiah suffered greatly on the Cross, but it was not suffering that the Torah required, but specifically death and death on a tree. Paul is most clear about this in Galatians chapter three.

Paul writes:

"For as many as are of works of Law are under a curse; for it has been written, 'cursed are all whom do not remain in all which have been written in the Book of the law and do them.'"

Galatians 3:10

Paul quotes here from a few different verses from the Book of Deuteronomy (Deut. 27:26, 28:58, 30:10) to substantiate his point. What he wants the reader to understand is that if one does not keep all the commandments, then this one is accursed and will experience death (not just physical, but also spiritual). In fact, physical death is one of the outcomes of spiritual death. Because of the consequence of original sin, it is impossible for a human to keep the Torah perfectly. It is in light of this that Paul continues and states:

> *"But that by means of Torah no one is made righteous
> before G-d is clear; but the righteous from faith will live.
> But the Law is not from faith; however the one who does
> them shall live in them"*
>
> Galatians 3:11-12

These verses are foundational to a proper understanding of
this chapter. Paul strongly affirms that justification (the process
of one being made righteous before G-d) is not achieved by
means of the Law. In regard to this point, he states that it is self-
evident to all. Christianity embraces this point and rightly so.
Next, Paul links together righteousness with faith. Here again,
Christianity would strongly affirm this and rightly so. At the end
of verse 11 Paul writes, *"the righteous of faith shall live." What
does he mean by this statement? In order to answer this question
one must* carefully read the next verse. He begins by stating,
"But the Law is not from faith." It is important to remember
that Paul began speaking about Abraham in verse six of this
third Chapter of Galatians and the primary subject is faith. The
chapter opens with Paul scolding the Galatians because they
are not walking in faith; rather they are starting to embrace
works of the Law. Wait a second, is this not where I am leading?
Absolutely not! There is a most significant difference that must
not be overlooked here. The Galatians were turning to embrace
the Law, i.e. works of the Law as an instrument for justification.
This is not the proper route to take for justification, rather, as
has been stated several times previously, it is faith, faith in the
grace of G-d.

Paul interjects Abraham into the discussion, because
Abraham is known as a man of faith. It is important to
remember that the Torah was not given to Israel until 430 years
after Abraham (See Galatians 3:17). This fact means that one
who is walking according to faith does not require the Torah.
Rather, the issue which is being stressed is that the Torah was
given to a faithless people.

Why was this? The answer is to manifest their faithlessness, which revealed itself in sin. It is for this reason that Paul correctly wrote, *"But the Law is not from faith,"* meaning that it was not because of the faithfulness of man that HaShem gave the Law. He concludes verse 12 by stating, *"However, the one who does them shall live in them."* It is this final sentence that Christianity, by and large, does not comprehend. In order to interpret these words properly, one must pay close attention to how this sentence begins. Paul chooses the Greek word, "ἀλλά." This word serves to introduce a thought or an idea which the author wishes to emphasize. It can as well point out to the reader a concept or idea which the author wishes to clarify.

Although Paul had just taught that the Law was not provided due to faithfulness; he does want to emphasize and clarify that the Torah commandments, when observed, provide a framework for one's life. In other words, Abraham did not have the Torah, yet because he was led by faith, he lived in a manner that reflected the righteousness of the Torah.

Today, believers are equipped with the Holy Spirit. Paul stated earlier that it was by means of faith that one receives the Holy Spirit (See Galatians 3:2). Why is this important? The answer is because when one lives according to the Holy Spirit, i.e. in faith, this same one fulfills the righteousness of the Law:

> *"In order that the righteous requirement of the Law should be fulfilled in us, the ones who not according to the flesh walk, rather according to the Spirit."*
>
> Romans 8:4

Because much of Christianity teaches that the Holy Spirit and the Law are antitheses of one another, the Church fails to connect the Torah with the character and nature of the Millennial Kingdom. Before dealing with the implications of Paul's words at the end of verse 12, and this last statement concerning the Church, let us first continue in this section of

Galatians and focus on the relationship between the Torah and the Cross.

Having learned that the Torah manifests one's unrighteousness and reveals this person as dead spiritually, and a recipient of G-d's future judgment, the logical person will seek redemption. It has been stated several times previously that the standard which HaShem uses to define righteousness is His Law; therefore, redemption must also be defined by the Torah. It is with this in mind that Paul proclaims:

> "*Messiah redeemed us from the curse of the Law having become for us accursed, because it has been written, 'cursed is everyone who is hung upon the tree.'*"
>
> Galatians 3:13

Paul uses Deuteronomy 21:23 to support his point. One must remember that there are two different, but related, ways to describe the Torah. Moses, as previously stated, speaks of the Law as "life and death" as well as "blessing and curse." Obviously there is a connection between "life" and "blessing" as well as "death" and "curse." Therefore, it is because Messiah died on the tree, i.e. the Cross, that He became accursed. Once again, it would not be enough just for Yeshua to die, His death needed to be on the Cross, so as to fulfill the full aspect of the condemnation which comes from the Torah. Because Yeshua was indeed hung on the tree, He paid the full measure of what might be called the negative aspect of the Torah (death and curse).

Now, by means of the redemption that He purchased on our behalf, something becomes a reality for the believer. It is to this new reality that Paul continues to speak. In the next verse, he writes about the blessing of Abraham. The word "*blessing*" is very important. Not only does the believer need not experience death (eternal separation and condemnation from G-d), but now, by means of the redemptive work of Messiah Yeshua, the promises made to Abraham can be experienced by each individual who responds to the Gospel in faith.

It is important for one to remember that earlier in this section (verse 11) Paul spoke of the relationship between faith and life. Only by means of faith, does one experience true life. Once again, the context is not simply a physical life, but rather a redemptive life, in which those who are declared righteous (just) by means of faith, will now live in such a way that they will express the righteousness of the Torah. As a result of this, they will reap blessing, for Paul wrote:

> "*In order that upon the Gentiles, the blessing of Abraham should come by means of Messiah Yeshua, in order that the promise of the Spirit, we should receive through the faith.*"
>
> Galatians 3:14

This verse is full of revelation. First of all, Gentiles are mentioned here. Many would ask the question that since Yeshua said He was sent to the lost sheep of the house of Israel, then why does Paul not refer to Israel? A very important truth to which is prophesied in the Hebrew Bible and supported by the New Testament is that the Messiah fulfills much of the work that Israel was called to do. It is necessary for one to remember the reason why HaShem brought Israel into existence in the first place.. The reason was in order to bring the blessing of Abraham upon the Gentiles. The blessing of Abraham must be understood in two separate, but highly related components.

The first is justification, that is, the forgiveness of sins. When an individual believes, i.e. exercises faith, he is declared righteous by G-d. Through Messiah's work of redemption, a covenantal relationship with HaShem is established. The second component is the actual entering into the Kingdom. Be aware that the Millennial Kingdom will not be established until Israel also responds to the Gospel. Therefore, stating that the blessing of Abraham comes upon the Gentiles is foundational to the Abrahamic covenant's original intent.

Next is that believers should receive the promise of the Spirit by faith. We have already learned that those who walk in faith, i.e. in the Spirit, fulfill the righteous requirements of the Law (Romans 8:4). Paul emphasizes that the true sons of Abraham (spiritually speaking) are those who live in faith like Abraham. The question which now must be answered is what do these things mean, practically speaking?

Torah Righteousness and the Believer Today

It is this area that is all but neglected by Christianity today and, because of this, it is hard for Christianity to speak in specific terms concerning the Millennial Kingdom. Once again, if one believes that the Torah is not related to righteousness and is a thing of the past, then what is this one to do with a Kingdom whose character and framework are expressed and defined by the righteousness of the Torah? Or with a Kingdom that is administered by the commandments of the Torah?

When one turns to prophetic passages that speak about the Millennial Kingdom which has a Temple and where sacrifices are offered, the normal response is to allegorize these passages or spiritualize them. Others prefer to explain them away by asserting that they speak about a previous time and therefore have been fulfilled or due to Israel's disobedience, they are rendered void and therefore to be understood as no longer applicable.

If the Torah is still relevant today, then one must answer the question of how exactly should believers apply the Law to their lives? The first point which has to be acknowledged is the nature of this current dispensation. Since 70 A.D., there has not been a Temple in Jerusalem. This fact makes it impossible to keep a large portion of the commandments.

James states in regard to the Torah:

"For whoever should keep the whole Law but should stumble
/ offend in one (place) he became guilty of all."

James 2:10

This verse informs the reader that the Torah must be
considered as a unit and not as 613 individual commandments.
If a person should break one of them or if he should fail to keep
one of them; then this person is considered to be a transgressor
of the entire Torah. This principle is also seen in Judaism. If a
Torah scroll should have just one of its letters written incorrectly,
or if even one letter has a small portion of it which has worn off
over time so that it is not complete, then the entire Torah scroll
is considered flawed and it cannot be used in the Synagogue
service. This is true even when reading from a section that does
not contain the word which has the flaw. Why is this relevant?
It is relevant to teach us that **the Torah is not "in force" today**.
This fact, however, does **not** mean that there is not any relevance
to the Torah today.

The Torah is still valuable in manifesting sin and showing
the need for redemption. Also, when believers study the Law
(each of the 613 Biblical commandments), under the guidance
and illumination of the Holy Spirit, with the intent of applying
the truth contained in each commandment to his life, then the
Torah can assist the believer in growing and maturing in faith
and deed. The Torah should not be utilized for the purpose of
judging or condemning another or as an instrument to exalt
one over another.

Rather, it ought to be used as a tool for self-examination
and introspection, whereby the believer can identify areas of
weakness and sinful tendencies in his life and understand better
G-d's expectations for His people. One might counter and say,
"Should not a believer do this with all of Scripture?" The answer
is, of course, yes indeed! However, the problem is that the Torah
is neglected by a significant percentage of believers today and
throughout Church history. This has caused believers to often

fail in maturing spiritually and to lack the influence and power that HaShem intended the body of Messiah (believers) to have in the world.

What will the Millennial Kingdom look like since the Torah will figure in so significantly? This is the subject of the next chapter.

Chapter 3

THE TORAH AND THE MILLENNIAL KINGDOM ACCORDING TO EZEKIEL

Anyone who has read the Gospels, quickly learns of Yeshua's emphasis on the Kingdom. It is safe to say that the Kingdom was not only important to Him, but the primary focus of His teaching. Obviously what is important to our L-rd should also be important to us. This is why it is so problematic that the vast majority of Christians today know so little about the Millennial Kingdom. Despite Yeshua's emphasis upon it, it is a topic which is seldom studied in most congregations. One of the places which describes this Kingdom in the greatest detail is the final section of Ezekiel's prophecy (Chapters 40-48). This section follows immediately after the war of Gog and Magog, which is also known as the battle of Armageddon.

These latter chapters of Ezekiel's prophecy follow a chronological order, for shortly after the war of Gog and Magog, the Millennial Kingdom will indeed begin. However, it is most

significant when the prophet received this vision of the Kingdom, that the text states:

> *"In the twenty-fifth year of our exile on the beginning of the
> year and the tenth day of the month in the fourteenth year
> after which the city was struck, on that very day was the
> Hand of the L-rd upon me..."*
>
> Ezekiel 40:1

The reader is told that 25 of the 70 years of exile had already
passed. Many people probably had lost hope that the Kingdom
of Israel would ever be established in Jerusalem again. Yet,
it was during this low point that the prophet was taken to
Israel in a vision. Before discussing this vision, it is highly
significant that the verse states that this vision was received
at the beginning of the year. Literally, the phrase is Rosh
HaShanah, like the rabbinical name of the Jewish holiday.
Although Biblically the Jewish New Year begins in the month
of Aviv, i.e. the Spring, the oral tradition of Judaism actually
speaks of four different New Years throughout the year. Each
one of these New Years relates to different aspects of Jewish
observance, such as tithing, fruits from trees, holidays, kings,
etc.

The Talmud understands this phrase to indeed relate to the
holiday of Rosh HaShanah, which takes place in the seventh
month (the Fall), and therefore sees great meaning in the fact
that the tenth day of this month is mentioned. This day then
would be Yom Kippur, the Day of Atonement. According to
Leviticus 25:8-13, there is an additional significance to this
date. This is because every fifty years on Yom Kippur the year of
Jubilee begins. Some of the primary aspects of the Jubilee year
are restoration and liberty. Hence, according to the Rabbis, there
is a strong relationship between the Kingdom and restoration.
This concept was also understood by the disciples, who asked
Yeshua:

"...Master, are You at this time restoring the Kingdom to Israel?"

Acts 1:6

This verse includes an interrogative particle which not only elicits an answer, but normally expresses a wish or desire. Hence, the disciples hoped that during their lifetime Yeshua would establish the Kingdom. The fact that their question specifically asked whether at that time the Kingdom was going to be restored to **Israel** had great significance. It is not the timing for establishing the Kingdom upon which I want to focus, rather the fact that they stated, "...**the Kingdom to Israel**". This statement confirms that they rightly understood that Israel, the Land and the Jewish people, will play a foundational role in this Kingdom. It is important to note that not only is restoration a major tenet of the Kingdom, but so also is redemption.

If one understands the phrase Rosh HaShanah in the Biblical sense, rather than the Talmudic (taking place in the Spring, rather than the Fall), then there is a major difference in regard to the significance of the tenth of the month being referenced by the verse. Scripture informs that the tenth of Nissan (Aviv) has special relevance concerning Passover (the Festival of Redemption). It was on this day that a Jewish family would bring the Passover lamb into their home:

"Speak to all the congregation of Israel saying, 'On the tenth day of this month, they shall take for themselves every man a lamb for the house of (the) patriarch, a lamb for a house.'"

Exodus 12:3

The tenth day of Nissan was when the preparations for the Passover sacrifice began. If Ezekiel's prophecy did indeed intend the reference to be the tenth of Nissan, rather than in the seventh month (Tishre), then this prophecy serves as not only a vision for the Kingdom, but also a call to make preparations for the Kingdom.

One is also told in Ezekiel 40:1 that this vision came to the prophet *"in the fourteenth year after which the city was struck"*. Usually the number fourteen is thought of as 2 sevens. The number seven relates to holiness, sanctification, and blessing. In other words, even though the Holy City of Jerusalem had been destroyed by the Babylonians, there was a purpose for this taking place. It was necessary to bring about a change, one which had been sanctified by HaShem and would reflect the Holiness of G-d, and in the end bless His people. The number 14 can be thought of as a double blessing or overflowing. It is very significant that Ezekiel did not simply see the Land of Israel in the vision, but the text explicitly states that he was brought to the Land of Israel. The importance of this is seen by the fact that the Scripture states this not just once but twice (See Ezekiel 40:1-2). Some understand this emphasis as relating to the future return of the Jewish people back to the Land of Israel as a necessary part of the final redemptive work of Messiah (taking place during His Second Coming). The text states that they were *"brought to the Land,"* implying that Messiah Yeshua will bring about the future Exodus in a similar manner as HaShem caused the first Exodus to take place, i.e. supernaturally.

Once Ezekiel arrives to Israel, he sees an angelic figure that is holding two things in his hand: a linen cord and a measuring rod. It becomes clear that the measurements, of the city and of the Temple, reveal important nuances about each of them. It is possible to do a fascinating study of these things, but for the purpose of this book, let it suffice to say that in the same way that one can speak about the character of an individual using the term stature, so too here are these measurements revealed in order to manifest certain traits and aspects concerning the places and things in the city and in the Temple. These measurements could be derived from the rod, so why is there also mentioned here the linen cord?

Some have pointed out that things such as round pillars could not have been measured by a measuring rod and a cord or "rope" would be more agile and would make it easier to measure such things. To this point I do not disagree; however, the fact that there is a unique word used for the cord rather than the basic Hebrew word "rope" is most significant. Instead of the normal Hebrew word which one would expect to appear here, it is most significant that the same word which was used to speak about "fringes" of a four corner garment (the tassels) appears in verse three as it does in the book of Numbers:

> "And HaShem spoke to Moses, saying, 'Speak to the Children of Israel and you shall say to them, make for themselves tassels upon the corners of their garments throughout their generations. And you shall place upon the tassel of each corner a blue **cord**. And it shall be for you for a tassel and when you shall look at it, you shall remember all the commandments of HaShem and you shall do them..."
>
> Numbers 15:37-39

In the book of Genesis the entire tassel is known by the same word I have translated as "cord" (See Genesis 38:18). It is clear from the passage from the book of Numbers that there is a special relationship between the tassel and the commandments of G-d. Hence, an additional reason why Ezekiel's prophecy contained the word "cord," and perhaps the primary reason, was to reveal to the reader that the Kingdom would reflect and be defined by the Holiness that is inherent to the Torah, i.e. the commandments of G-d.

Ezekiel is very specific about the various places and vessels which he describes beginning in chapter forty and verse five. In fact, he spends nearly three full chapters on this subject. As previously stated, there is much significance in these measurements; however, for our purposes we shall press on to what the prophet reveals in chapter 43. Here, in this section,

Ezekiel introduces to the reader a special individual, one whom the Jewish sages have debated the identity of for over 2,500 years. This one is known as "the Prince."

Also beginning in chapter 43 there is a clear emphasis on the eastern gate. This is the gate, according to Jewish tradition, that the Messiah will enter through when He returns to Jerusalem at the end of this age. The prophet states:

> *"And then he (an angel, the same angel as is mentioned in 40:3) led me to the gate which turns to the way of the east. And behold, the glory of the G-d of Israel came from the way of the east and His voice as the voice of many waters and the Land was illuminated from His glory."*
>
> Ezekiel 43:1-2

Ezekiel relates to the reader in the next few verses that this vision was very similar to what he had seen prior to the destruction of Jerusalem and the Babylonian captivity. For it was at that previous time that the glory of G-d had departed by way of the eastern gate; however, now this same glory is returning through it and fills the Temple. It is also revealed to Ezekiel that the Temple is where the throne of G-d shall be established and from there, He will dwell with the Children of Israel forever. Furthermore, whereas in the past the Children of Israel defiled themselves with idolatry and other sinful practices, now in the Millennial Kingdom they will no longer defile His Holy Name. Although we skipped over the nearly three chapters that contained the description of Jerusalem and the Temple area in the Millennial Kingdom, Ezekiel is told the following:

> *"You, O Son of Man, tell the house of Israel about the Temple and they shall be ashamed from their iniquities and they must measure the plan."*
>
> Ezekiel 43:10

The manner in which the Temple is designed actually manifests the holiness and glory of G-d. What the prophet wants to reveal to the reader is that when the Children of Israel understand the structure and nature of the Temple, they will be convicted of their sin. In other words, the Temple itself will also be an instrument of repentance. No sooner than stating these things, then the text moves into a discussion of the altar and some of the sacrifices that will occur there. The fact that there will be sacrifices during the Millennial Kingdom is quite problematic for many believers. After all, is not Yeshua's death on the Cross the sacrifice that ended the need for any additional sacrifices to be made?

There is no question that Yeshua's death is absolutely sufficient for the total forgiveness of one's sins. His blood, and only His blood, provides what HaShem requires for a sinner to be eternally redeemed. This being the case, then why should there be a need for any additional sacrifices during the Millennial Kingdom? This question poses a difficult dilemma for many Christians, so much so that they prefer to ignore this latter portion of Ezekiel's prophecy altogether or spiritualize it in such a manner that they rob it of any future relevance.

Sacrifices and the Millennial Kingdom

When dealing with the sacrifices which will take place during the Millennial Kingdom, it is crucial to remember two important points concerning the Millennium. First, who will be residing in this Kingdom and secondly, what is the overall purpose of the Millennial Kingdom. Both of these things have already been mentioned. The inhabitants consist of three groups: first, those who took part in the Rapture; second, both Jews and Gentiles who came to faith in Messiah Yeshua after the Rapture; and finally, those born during the Millennial Kingdom. As previously stated, those who took part in the Rapture will have received a glorified heavenly body and will not take part personally in the offering of any sacrifices. This group will rule and reign with Messiah Yeshua and will act in a supervisory role (See Revelation 20:4-6).

During the Millennial Kingdom, Messiah Yeshua will dwell in Jerusalem and His presence and authority will be known by all Kingdom inhabitants. In a similar way to this, the prophet Isaiah states:

"...for every eye shall see when HaShem returns to Zion."
Isaiah 52:8

Individuals therefore will actually see Yeshua ruling from Jerusalem and will know that He has absolute authority. This is one of the implications of the statement that He rules with a rod of iron. In other words, His rule is **absolute** to the fullest extent of the word, so that any and all violations of His authority (laws) will be met with an immediate response by Him. The question, "Do you believe in Messiah Yeshua?" will have a vastly different application in the Millennial Kingdom. No longer will this question be related to faith, in the sense of believing in something you cannot see. Rather, Yeshua will be visible to all in the Millennial Kingdom and His rule will be undeniable. The idea of faithfulness will be expected to express itself as obedience during the Millennial Kingdom. One will not simply be required to profess a belief; rather he will have to act in obedience to the Torah, i.e. the Law that will govern the Millennial rule of Yeshua.

It is important for one to remember that obedience to the Torah also includes that when one sins and violates a Torah commandment, certain actions must be taken. The Torah contains grace, and admonishes the violator to demonstrate his repentance by offering a sacrifice. Prior to the redemptive work of Messiah Yeshua on the Cross, these sacrifices served two purposes. The first was to keep G-d's judgement at bay until Messiah should come and complete the work of redemption.

The second was to point to Messiah's work of redemption which involved Him actually becoming the sacrifice for ALL SIN. Hence, in the same way that those sacrifices and offerings pointed to Messiah prior to His Coming, those that will take place during the Millennial Kingdom will point back to His death on the Cross.

The strict administration of Torah Law that Yeshua will enforce serves to manifest the righteousness of His Kingdom. It is vital for one not to forget that during the Millennium there will be an astronomical number of people being born, all of which will have to be taught the righteousness of Messiah. As stated previously, Scripture identifies the Torah as the tool which HaShem provided in the past in order to assist humanity to identify that which is righteous according to G-d and the same will be true during the Millennial Kingdom. Once again, it is the failure of most of Christianity to understand that the righteousness of the Law and the righteousness of Messiah are, in fact, the same righteousness, which has caused the Church to err in its understanding of many of the major tenets of the Millennial Kingdom.

When Ezekiel begins to speak concerning the laws of the altar, he mentions the Priests, but not all of them. Rather, only those who are of the seed of Zadok (See Ezekiel 43:19). The question that needs to be raised is: why are only those who are descendants of this priestly family taken to serve in the Millennial Kingdom? When one examines the Biblical record of Zadok, a few interesting points are found. Zadok's name is derived from the Hebrew word meaning "righteous." He was a direct descendant of the priest Pinchas, who was known for his zeal for righteousness and stood fast against idolatry (See Numbers 25:1-19). Zadok also was zealous for righteousness and opposed the paganism which plagued Israel. He and the priests under his rule remained loyal to David when others rebelled and followed Avshalom, David's son. He also was the one who anointed Solomon. Solomon is linked allegorically to the Messiah, for a well-known term for the Messiah is "Ben David", meaning the son of David. It was due to all of these reasons that the sages of old, as well as Ezekiel, understood that Zadok's descendants would play a significant role in the Millennial Temple.

The first order of business for the descendants of Zadok will be the cleansing of the Temple. This cleansing will involve a seven day period. It is most significant that the reader is told that it will be from the eighth day forward that sacrifices may be offered upon the altar. The number eight relates to "newness". What is new about these sacrifices? At the end of the chapter one reads, "...*and I will accept you, says the L-rd G-d*" (Ezekiel 43:27). Whereas the sacrifices in the First and Second Temples were primarily ceremonial, those offerings in the Millennial Temple will have greater spiritual implications for those who offer them.

It has already been stated that there is a special significance to the eastern gate. One learns that while the other gates function normally, the eastern gate is usually closed. In fact Ezekiel states:

> "*And HaShem said to me, 'This gate shall be closed, it shall not be opened and no man shall enter through it, for HaShem the G-d of Israel entered through it and it shall be closed.*"
>
> Ezekiel 44:2

This verse is likely a reference to what was stated earlier, namely that at the time of the Babylonian exile, HaShem departed from the Temple and from Jerusalem through this gate. It is clear that this gate has a special status attached to it. No sooner than Ezekiel reminds us of this, he says:

> "*The Prince, a prince is he; he will sit in it (the gate) to eat bread before HaShem; from the way of the hall of the gate he will come in and from its way he shall go out.*"
>
> Ezekiel 44:3

It is clear that the location where the Prince sits has a special connection to HaShem and the fact that he eats bread in this same location is most informing. The eating of bread has a special significance in the Bible and points to a communion between those who partake together. The text states that the Prince will eat bread *before HaShem*! What exactly this special connection is between the Prince and HaShem has been debated by the rabbinical sages for centuries. Rashi, for example, states that the Prince is the High Priest; while others have conjectured that he is the Messiah (See the Metzudot). There are serious problems with the view that the Prince in this section of Ezekiel (chapters 44, 45, & 46) is the Messiah. (Please note that the Prince in Ezekiel chapter 37:25 is most certainly the Messiah). Although much could be said concerning this Prince, let us move on for now to the next thing that Ezekiel reveals, the glory of the L-rd filling the Temple.

The glory of HaShem filling the Temple is a condition that will characterize the Millennial Kingdom. This fact points to two truths which the reader should learn. The first is that the Millennial Kingdom will be distinguished from this current age by G-d's glory clearly being manifested from Jerusalem, which confirms HaShem's presence among His people. There are, of course, those who want to counter this point and argue that the glory of G-d is manifested through the lives of believers today, for we are a Temple of the Holy Spirit (See 1 Corinthians 6:19-20). While this point is true, Ezekiel is speaking about a revealing of HaShem's glory not because of any behavior of His people, but because G-d is dwelling in the Temple in a unique manner. This is similar to saying that all believers are sons of G-d, but it is Yeshua Who is the Son of G-d! There will be a special status given to the Temple area that currently in this age does not exist.

The second truth is that HaShem's righteous rule is also a cause for His glory being manifested. When Ezekiel beholds this glory filling the Temple, the text informs the reader that he was brought to the northern gate, to the front of the Temple (See Ezekiel 44:4). This location has a special significance according to Jewish tradition. Scholars who specialize in matters related to the Sanhedrin state:

> "The Sanhedrin met in a building known as Lishkat Ha-Gazith or the Hall of Hewn Stones, which has been placed by many scholars as built into the North wall of the Temple Mount," (The Sanhedrin.org).

Hence, one could rightly derive from the text that when Ezekiel peered into the Temple area and saw the glory of G-d filling it, it was because he was on the northern side. According to this tradition, he was actually looking into the part of the Temple that housed the Sanhedrin. Once again the emphasis is on the righteous rule that will characterize the Millennial Kingdom.

For those individuals who reject the future reality of the Millennial Kingdom, the next verse poses an insurmountable problem. Ezekiel is told to pay attention with both his eyes and ears to what is being revealed to him concerning the Temple statutes and laws. It is no accident that after being confronted by the Holiness of the Millennial Temple, the prophet is then commanded to speak to the house of Israel. Whereas Israel, during the Millennial Kingdom, will express the glory of G-d, during the actual time that Ezekiel lived, nothing could have been further from the truth. HaShem related to Israel as a rebellious nation who had indulged in numerous abominations (See Ezekiel 44:5-7). Hence, those who attempt to interpret this section, which speaks of Israel expressing the glory of G-d as applying to the past, cannot overcome the uniqueness of this passage, and the fact that it must point to the future.

This section continues, and there is a clear emphasis on those who are uncircumcised. It is vital for the reader to understand the terminology which the Hebrew text is using. Many English translations in this section speak about "strangers" or "foreigners." The Hebrew phrase that appears here relates to those who are **not** of Jewish descent. The passage reveals that HaShem is disturbed because these non-Jews are not circumcised. Why would HaShem be upset, knowing that non-Jews are not required to be circumcised? Such a question is in line with the position of Judaism today which believes that circumcision is only for Jewish individuals, but it certainly does not reflect G-d's desires for the Kingdom.

Rabbinical Judaism teaches that there is one set of laws (The Torah) for those who are descendants of Jacob, i.e. the Jewish people, and a different set of laws (Seven Noahide laws) for Gentiles. Rabbinical Judaism is most dogmatic that the Torah is absolutely forbidden for Gentiles. If a Gentile should want to follow the Torah, he must first convert and become rabbinically Jewish, and only after his conversion is completed, may he then begin to obey the Law. Judaism desires to keep strict distinction between Jewish individuals and Gentiles in one's religious practices. The question which must be raised is whether this distinction is Biblically correct?

When examining the Scripture and looking at those who HaShem states are His people from a Kingdom perspective, it is clear that they are from every tribe, language, and nation. In other words, there seems to be peoples from all types of backgrounds and ethnicities who are His people. Ezekiel reveals that HaShem is displeased because Gentiles are not obeying the same laws as the Jewish people. It is clear that in the Kingdom, Gentiles are not forced to become "Jewish," nor do they lose their identity as being from whatever ethnic background from which they were born, yet they are called to obey the same Torah as those from a Jewish background. The proper conclusion is that there is one Law for all people. HaShem did not give the Torah to the Jewish people so that the lifestyle it demands only be practiced by those of Jewish descent; rather G-d entrusted the Jewish people with the Torah so that they should practice it and in doing so become a "light to the Gentiles" and lead them to practice the same lifestyle based in the same Torah commandments.

What then about the Noahide laws? These seven commandments, which establish a lifestyle for non-Jews, are solely the creation of man. Although these laws are derived from the Scriptures, never do the Scriptures present them as a unit, nor as a basis for how Gentiles are to order their religious practices. Some have tried to interpret James' words at the Jerusalem Council as pertaining to the Noahide laws:

> *"Therefore I judge not to trouble those from the Gentiles turning to G-d; rather send to them to abstain from the defilement of idols, and sexual immorality, and from strangled (animals) and from blood. For Moses from generations of old in each city has those proclaiming him in the Synagogues each and every Shabbat being read."*
>
> Acts 15:19-21

James' words do not, in any way, validate the Noahide laws as a Biblically accepted manner of life for non-Jewish individuals who want to serve G-d and who believe in Messiah Yeshua. Many Christian theologians understand the Jerusalem Council as providing the Apostles' perspective on requirements for Gentile believers (after their salvation experience). Such a view does not reflect the context of this passage of Scripture. It is important for the reader to remember the primary issue that the council was addressing. The council addressed a salvation matter and not a lifestyle issue. The council met because certain men, who were from Jerusalem and part of the "believing community," had been following Paul and teaching those Gentiles who accepted the Gospel, that they were not truly saved until they were circumcised (See Acts 15:1-2). Hence, the issue was, does one have to be circumcised, in addition to faith in the Gospel, in order to be justified (saved)?

Furthermore, it was also stated by the same individuals that Gentiles needed to be commanded to keep the Law of Moses:

"But stood up certain ones from the sect of the Pharisees having believed; saying: 'That it is necessary to circumcise them and to command also to keep the Law of Moses.'"

Acts 15:5

Peter, Paul, and Barnabas spoke to these matters and disagreed with the believing Pharisees, testifying how HaShem had moved mightily among the Gentiles as the result of the preaching of the Gospel, without having circumcised them. It was James, as the elder of the believing community, who rendered the conclusion on this matter. His statement does not relate to conduct for Gentile believers after a salvation experience, but provides a basis for with whom it is permissible to share the Gospel. James' remarks are not shaped by the Noahide laws, which may not have even existed, as a theological unit during the time of the latter Second Temple period. The earliest recording of them appears in the Talmud in maseket Sanhedrin 56a (Fourth to fifth century AD).

The issue is whether the Gospel can be given to one who is uncircumcised or does this person need to be first circumcised, then the Gospel can be presented. In reality, the Gospel can be discussed prior to circumcision, but according to the "believing" sect of Pharisees, the acceptance of the Gospel was only after circumcision had been performed. They were most adamant about the order, first circumcision and then the receiving of Yeshua for redemption.

James' requirements: *to abstain from the defilement of idols, and sexual immorality, and from strangled (animals) and from blood*, related to the major characteristics of idolatry. In other words, there was a concern that the Gentiles, who were idol worshippers, would simply add Yeshua as another one of their objects of worship. It was because of this, that James gave these requirements, in order to make sure that a Gentile had left idolatry before receiving Yeshua as L-rd. Perhaps an example would help clarify the matter.

It is clear in the Scripture that homosexuality is a sin. Can a homosexual be saved? Yes, providing that he acknowledges that such behavior is a violation of G-d's will and he desires to be set free of this sin, as well as all other sins. One is, of course, not saved by deeds, all believers struggle with sin. The desire to leave sin is not particular to the homosexuals; all people, when receiving the Gospel, must desire to turn away from sin. The point which James is simply emphasizing is that idolatry and the Gospel are incompatible with one another. James clearly rejects the view that physical circumcision is in any way a requirement for salvation.

In regard to the Law of Moses, it is most significant that James does not say anything about it as a precondition for a salvation experience. However, he does state, *"For Moses from generations of old in each city has those proclaiming him in the Synagogues each and every Shabbat being read."* Only at this point does the issue of lifestyle after receiving the Gospel enter into the discussion. James does not mandate any specific observance for Gentile believers, but there is a clear expectation that Gentile believers would be attending the synagogue for worship. And there they would hear the Torah being read each week and under the leadership of the Holy Spirit they would apply the word of G-d to their lives. Again, it is very important that there is no mandate from James concerning the commandments as to what they shall or shall not do; rather there is only the expectation that all believers would be exposed to the Scripture. Obviously two thousand years ago, individuals did not own a personal copy of the Bible and there was a clear need to attend a synagogue to hear the word of G-d. However, there are some additional factors for why James would instruct Gentile believers to hear the Law of Moses. It is quite reasonable to conclude that James said this because there is relevance in the Torah for the believer (Jew and Gentile). Second, Jewish individuals and Gentiles worshipping together should be considered the norm and will be the norm in the Millennial Kingdom.

It is clear that the Millennial Temple is a house of worship for all peoples (Isaiah 56:7). There is maintained a distinction in one's identity, that is, whether one be Jewish or a Gentile, but all people, regardless of ethnicity are called to live by the same standard of obedience and be G-d's people. It is for this reason that it is revealed to Ezekiel that HaShem is angry that there are Gentiles who are uncircumcised in the Temple. Why is circumcision singled out?

Circumcision is usually associated with the Law of Moses; however, it is important to note that circumcision has its origin with Abraham. Why should Abraham, the man of faith, be associated with circumcision? Circumcision should rightly be understood as the removal of flesh. When flesh is removed from the body it dies. Hence, it is proper to conclude that the theological message of circumcision is the death of the flesh by means of faith. Because one is called to worship the L-rd in Spirit and Truth, there is no place for the manifestation of the flesh in the Temple.

HaShem instructs Ezekiel to speak the following words:

> "*And say to (the) rebellious, to the House of Israel, 'Thus said the L-rd G-d, abundant is all your abominations O House of Israel,*"
>
> Ezekiel 44:6

Clearly, the numerous amounts of sinful acts mentioned here are the results of the flesh. Therefore, HaShem immediately points out that there are uncircumcised individuals in the Temple area. Many would argue that those who are called uncircumcised are those who are uncircumcised in the heart. This idea is rooted in the tendency among many to allegorize and spiritualize passages rather than taking them literally. Such a position, however, cannot be taken here, as the next verse states:

*"...when you brought Gentiles, uncircumcised ones in heart and **uncircumcised in flesh** to be in My Temple to defile My House..."*

Ezekiel 44:7

It is obvious that HaShem is displeased with those uncircumcised Gentiles who entered into the sacred area to worship. However, it is most significant that those who are held accountable for this violation are the Levities, for one reads:

"Rather the Levites which distanced (themselves) from Me with the straying of Israel who strayed after idols; they shall bear their iniquity."

Ezekiel 44:10

What is the intent of this verse in light of its context? Ezekiel is being informed that the guilt for uncircumcised Gentiles being in the Temple and offering sacrifices is upon the Levites. Why should this be? One learns from Scripture that the Levites, as well as the Priests, had the responsibility for teaching the Torah (See 2 Chronicles 30:22, 35:3, Nehemiah 8:7). Therefore, because Israel did not follow the Torah properly, they did not have the influence on the Gentiles so that they knew how to worship G-d correctly. In actuality, what this passage reveals is that it was the Israelites, under the leadership of the Levites, who had embraced the idolatry of the Gentiles. Such behavior on the part of Israel was unfortunately most common throughout much of her history.

However, one priestly family remained faithful; they were the descendants of Zadok. It was due to their faithfulness that they received the charge to be over Temple worship in the Millennial Kingdom. When one closely examines what the second half of chapter 44 states concerning the priests in the Millennial Kingdom, he finds there is great similarity between them and what one reads in the Torah in regard to the priests who served in the Tabernacle. It is very significant that the term "prince" is used in regard to the priests. This adds credence to the **Prince** who was mentioned earlier in this same chapter, being the High Priest.

It is also in the Millennial Kingdom where the priests will instruct the people in regard to those things which are sacred and those things which are profane. They will not only teach the commandments, but also keep charge of the appointed times, i.e. Shabbat and Festival Days. Why would these appointed times be important during the Millennial? First, one needs to remember that during the Millennial all things will be regulated by Torah Law. Second, Shabbat and Festivals are inherently related to the Kingdom. Such a view is not only accepted by Judaism, but also Paul writes about this in Colossians chapter two:

> *"Therefore, do not let anyone judge you in food and in drink or in regard to a Festival or New Month celebration or Shabbat; which are a shadow of the things which are about to be, but the substance is of the Messiah."*
>
> Colossians 2:16-17

These two verses help to clarify that indeed the Torah and the Kingdom are closely related. Paul takes major elements of the Law in verse 16, kashrut (the dietary laws) and the appointed times, i.e. the holy days (Shabbat, Rosh Chodesh and the Festivals) and he teaches that these create a shadow. What exactly is this shadow? The answer is *"the things which are about to be."* Most English translations render this phrase as "the things which are coming." Although the Greek phrase "τῶν μελλόντων" is more properly rendered with the word "about," rather than "coming," the main concept is found in both translations, namely that the verse is speaking about something taking place in the future. The nuance that translating the Greek in the most literal manner provides is that "τῶν μελλόντων" contains an added emphasis on the potential nearness of that which is about to be. What is about to be or what is coming? The answer is that which is inherently related to the Messiah. This is because the shadow which was cast is of the Messiah. In order to help one understand this in simpler terms, I will paraphrase the passage:

> {*Therefore, do not let anyone judge you because you observe (or do not observe) the dietary laws or a Festival or celebrate a new Jewish month or the Sabbath day; for these things only reveal that which is about to happen, it is the Messiah Who is the true representation of these things!*}

An important question which must be asked is what exactly is about to happen or, stated differently, what is coming? The answer is the **Kingdom**. Each festival, for example, has a unique aspect to it which points, not only to the Person and the Work of Messiah Yeshua in a particular manner, but also to a specific aspect of the Kingdom.

It is hard to comprehend that so many Christian theologians fail to see the connection between the Torah and the Kingdom. In fact, some may not fail to see it; they simply may refuse to acknowledge it. A good example of this is the New International Version translation of the Bible (NIV) and the theological biases which this translation reflects. When rendering Colossians 2:17, the NIV has the following:

> "*These are a shadow of things that were to come; the reality, however, is found in Christ.*"

The problem here is that the phrase "*that were to come*" clearly implies a change has taken place. The Greek language is most specific and there is absolutely no way to render this Greek phrase as, "*that were to come.*" The NIV provides such a rendering because it wants to reject any notion that things related to the Torah have any place or role in the future. Therefore, they willfully mistranslate the Greek phrase, "τῶν μελλόντων." It is quite obvious that it was willfully mistranslated because the phrase is found in the present tense (present active participle) and not in the imperfect tense, which the word "**were**" (as in "*were to come*") would require.

The NIV translation, like many Christian theologians, is so determined to protect its theological positions that it does not hesitate to alter Scripture. In addition to this, those who worked on the NIV translation failed to give proper consideration to the implications of their actions. In the first half of the verse, those things relating to the Torah are presented as a shadow. In the latter half of the verse, that which casts the shadow is Messiah. It is clear, as stated previously, there is an inherent relationship between Messiah and these things which are about to be. The faulty translation of the NIV infers that G-d had intended certain things to be, but now they will not be (*that were to come*). Since it was indeed the Messiah Whom this shadow ultimately represents, how can this shadow change? Would not the change in the shadow imply that Messiah Himself would have to be altered? Naturally, this is not possible.

When one examines the context for this passage from Colossians chapter two, he finds that Paul is warning against the vain philosophy of man and earthly traditions. He calls them the rudiments of the world and states that they are highly inferior to that of the Messiah. For only in Messiah Yeshua is the power to be redeemed found. It is important for the reader to identify that Paul makes a distinction between these things, which he later calls the commandments and doctrines of men (See verse 22) and the commandments of G-d, which are referenced in verse 16. In regard to the commandments and doctrines of men Paul writes:

"On one hand they are reckoned to have wisdom in human devised "worship" and (in the) meager mindset (of humanity) and (in) the restraining of the body. On the other hand (they do not have) any value for bringing to an end the flesh."

Colossians 2:23

The message of this verse is that though human doctrines and practices may contain what those of mere human intellect may view as spiritual, wise, and displaying discipline; such philosophies and practices do absolutely nothing to bring victory over the carnal nature of man in his fallen state. Only the Gospel of Messiah is able to defeat sin and bring salvation to humanity.

In this chapter, there are three things which Paul discusses— the traditions of man, the commandments of G-d, and the superiority of Messiah. In the previous paragraph, the insufficiencies of the traditions of man were discussed. In regard to the commandments of G-d, although they point to the Kingdom and reflect the righteousness of G-d, they, in and of themselves, cannot bring about any spiritual change in the condition of man. Rather, it is only Messiah Who can bring about the changes to humanity whereby one is prepared for life in the Kingdom. Let us now return to Ezekiel's prophecy.

When one enters into chapter 45, he reads of two sacred allotments of land which are divided into several portions. These various allotments are for the Temple, the Holy of Holies, and for the houses of those who serve in the Temple, both Priests and Levites. As one continues to read, it becomes most clear that this same framework is what the Children of Israel were called to follow prior to the Millennium, but failed. However, now, in the Millennial Kingdom, it will be scrupulously followed.

Chapter 47 contains a very informing vision which aids the reader to understand further implications concerning the Kingdom. The chapter opens up with Ezekiel (in a vision) being brought to the entrance of the Temple. There he noticed that there was water going forth from underneath the threshold of the Temple, flowing to the east. The text emphasizes that the water went down from below the right side of the Temple, south of the altar. Ezekiel is then taken out of the Temple by way of the northern gate, around once again to the eastern gate where he still sees water flowing from the right side. There are a few different words in Biblical Hebrew that could have been used to describe the water's movement. It is therefore significant that none of these words were chosen by the Prophet; rather the word which was chosen only occurs here (Ezekiel 47:2). This fact relates to the uniqueness of this event.

The word הכיפ not only describes the water gushing forth, but also welling up. As this vision continues, a man with a measuring rod is seen moving to the east. He begins to measure the distance from the Temple in thousand cubit increments. One would expect the depth of the water to be decreasing as he moves further eastward, however the opposite occurs. In order to emphasize this phenomenon, Ezekiel is asked, "*Have you seen?*"

When Ezekiel returns to the bank of the river, he notices a great tree on both sides of the river. Translations of the Hebrew usually render the phrase by placing the word "*tree*" in the plural; however the Hebrew has it in the singular. Logic demands that there be more than one tree since it is seen on both sides of the river bank. So why does not the Hebrew have the word "*tree*" in the plural? Logic also demands that the water would become shallower away from its source, yet this was not what occurred. One explanation is that the manner in which the tree is recorded in the Scripture places an emphasis on the tree. The concept of tree in the Bible relates to "fruitfulness" or "blessing." The most famous tree in the Hebrew Scriptures is the Tree of Life. As one continues to read in this section, the water which was flowing eastward enters into the sea. This sea is of course the Dead Sea. When these waters arrive at the Dead Sea they bring about a most significant change.

The reader is told that the waters (Dead Sea) are healed. The outcome of this healing is that now there will be life in the Dead Sea. Wherever these waters (from the Temple) will flow, they will bring about life. Whereas initially one reads only about one river, in verse 9 Ezekiel speaks of rivers:

> "*And it shall be every living creature which will swarm to which will **rivers** come there, will live; and there will be very many fish, for these will come to there and the waters will be healed; and will live all which will come to there **the river**.*"
>
> Ezekiel 47:9

Obviously the translation of this section of the verse is so literal it is hard to make sense from it. The tendency is to make the translation conform to that which is easily understood. This however is an error. Passages in the Scripture which are difficult to comprehend in the natural way they are written are done so for a reason. The reason is so that the reader must pause and struggle with the text in order to arrive at the proper interpretation. In this verse the same word which I translated "*river*" appears both in the singular and the plural. What is the reason for this? The verse is linked to Genesis 1:20, and in both of these verses (from Ezekiel and Genesis) there is a similar phrase:

> "*...the waters shall swarm with living creature...*"
>
> Genesis 1:20

> "*...every living creature which will swarm to which will **rivers** come there,*"
>
> Ezekiel 47:9

It is clear from the Genesis passage that the verse has to do with creation. This is also what Ezekiel wants the reader to understand, namely that one should view the Millennial

Kingdom as a second creation. When examining the verse from Ezekiel, one notices a few interesting observations. One reads in Genesis that there was one river flowing out of the Garden of Eden. Then the reader is told that this river divided into four rivers. The word for "river" is the standard Hebrew word for river. In the Ezekiel passage, the word for "river" is a different word entirely. This word first appears in the plural and then it appears in the singular. It is most significant that the word translated "river" in Ezekiel is derived from the same word which means "to inherit." The word usually refers to a river bed which at times may be empty and at other times may be flowing with water. Since verse nine was previously translated in a literal manner, let's render it in a way that explains its intent:

> " And it will be in the future, that every living creature which moves that the rivers shall come into contact will live; and there will be very many fish, for these rivers will flow and arrive to the location of the Dead Sea and the waters there will be healed; in fact this will be the outcome for everything which comes into contact with the river."

As one reads this verse, it should stand out that at first Ezekiel speaks about every living creature, and then he singles out fish. What could be the reason for this? Genesis 48:15-16 should be understood as a Messianic Blessing. In this section, Jacob is blessing the two sons of Joseph, Manasseh and Ephraim. The blessing speaks of the one sent by HaShem to redeem Jacob from all evil. The blessings begin by mentioning Abraham. Abraham is associated with faith, but faith in exactly what? The answer is faith in the promises of G-d. The greatest promise of G-d is Messiah and the redemption He offers. When Jacob blesses the two sons of Joseph he says:

> "...May the G-d Whom our fathers walked before Him, Abraham and Isaac; the G-d who shepherds me even to this

*day. The Messenger Who redeems me from all evil, may
He bless the youths and may My Name be called in them,
the name of my fathers, Abraham and Isaac and may they
become fish in abundance in the midst of the land."*

Genesis 48:15-16

Although most English translations do not render the
Hebrew properly, the text does indeed read, *"and may they
become fish in abundance in the midst of the land"*. The word
"fish" is most important. It is this verse and the ancient
understanding of it that was the reason why Yeshua, when
He called His disciples said, *"Follow Me and I will make you
fishers of men."* Fish also represent in Jewish understanding,
the concept of blessing. It is traditional, for example, to have
a fish head on one's table during the Rosh HaShannah meal,
signifying a blessed New Year. Fish are also linked to the
Christian faith as a symbol of Messiah and the Kingdom of
blessing that He will establish.

Fish were singled out in Ezekiel's vision to point to these
events occurring in the Messianic Age and describing the
blessed nature of this age. There are three descriptive events
which take place in this prophecy that assist the reader in
understanding the nature of the Millennial Kingdom. They are
"healing," "abundance," and "life." It has already been stated that,
when the river of water which flows from the Temple touches
the waters of the Dead Sea, the waters there are healed (verses
8 and 9). Likewise, we have seen that the same river gives life
to every living creature it touches (verse 9). Finally, when
speaking about the fish, the reader is informed that there will
be an abundant amount of species of fish as well as an abundant
amount of fish (verses 9 and 10).

When studying further into this vision, the emphasis on the
river continues. It is said that on both sides of the river there
will be every type of tree that is good for food. These trees have
some characteristics which are quite different from trees in

this dispensation. What is the connection between the river, its water and the trees? What is unique about the leaves of the trees? These question and others will be investigated in the next chapter.

Chapter 4

THE FEAST OF TABERNACLES AND THE KINGDOM

In the previous chapter, there was an allusion between the river that flowed out of the Garden of Eden and the one that flowed out of the Temple. Although it was pointed out that in the book of Genesis the river was initially one river that became four, while in Ezekiel the river was first mentioned in the plural and then became singular, nothing was said about why this was the case or what possible significance these events had. In this chapter, an explanation will be presented that speaks not only to this issue, but also to the other matters raised at the end of the previous chapter.

The primary interest of this book is the Millennial Kingdom; yet to assist the reader in his comprehension of it, it is necessary at times to place Kingdom occurrences in light of historical events that have taken place. One of the best ways to understand many of the things that will characterize the Kingdom is to interpret them in light of what Scripture reveals about the Garden of Eden. As was discussed, the river that went forth from the Garden became four rivers. In actuality, the verse from Genesis does not say four "*rivers*," but four heads, as in headwaters. The word "*head*" in Hebrew can also be understood as "*first*," in the sense as the origin of something. The Hebrew word which is translated as "*Genesis*" is derived from this same word. What needs to be emphasized here is that in the Garden of Eden the one river divided into four, whereas in Ezekiel the rivers will return and become only one. Why just one? The answer is that in the Kingdom there is an emphasis on the concept of "one." This concept will be developed further in the next section.

The Feast of Tabernacles has many important elements, one of which is water. At the end of the festival there is a special prayer for water. It is the prophet Zechariah who links together the Feast of Tabernacles with the Kingdom. He clearly states that the end of this age will be brought about when Messiah Yeshua returns, as promised, to the Mount of Olives. Zechariah speaks of many different happenings when Messiah's feet land on the Mount of Olives. Most English translations speak of the day when this will occur as a "unique" day; however, in the Hebrew it states "*one day.*" This is also the exact phrase in Genesis 1:5, however, once again the English fails to render the Hebrew accurately and states the "*first day.*" It is vital to render the text as the Holy Spirit inspired it, in order that one may understand its revelation. The point is that the Millennial Kingdom should rightly be recognized as a Kingdom that manifests the original intent of G-d for His creation. This is why the number one appears frequently, in order to inform the reader that the Millennial Kingdom is moving toward the beginning, or in other words, to HaShem's original purposes.

The Hebrew word "*one*" is also the root for which the Hebrew word "*unity*" or "*oneness*" is derived. The idea that is being revealed here is that the Millennial Kingdom is characterized by the unity between HaShem and His creation. The outcome of this is the manifestation of His glory. The uniqueness of this day is seen in the following verse:

> "*And it shall come about on that day there will not be light XXXX XXXX.*"
>
> Zechariah 14:6

I did not translate the ending of this verse because of the various views concerning its meaning. The phase is either one or two Hebrew roots; it is either אפק or הרק or רקי or a combination of two of them. Perhaps the best way to understand what is being said in this verse is to continue to the next verse. There it is stated that:

> "*And it shall be one day, it will be known to HaShem, neither day nor night, and it shall be at the time of the evening, there will be light.*"
>
> Zechariah 14:7

From this verse it would seem that there will be a new reality for the Millennial Kingdom in regard to its light. The light in the Millennium will be different from the light of today. In addition, there does not appear to be any difference in the amount of light that shines in the day and the amount that is present in the night. Because there is no change from day to night, one might say that the condition is "*frozen.*" One of the words which I did not translate is in its corrected form ואפקי which is derived from the Hebrew word which means "*frozen.*" In order to assist one in understanding why light is so important to Zechariah, one needs to remember what is said in Genesis chapter one.

The original condition of the world was empty and void (See Genesis 1:2); however, by the end of the first chapter of Genesis, HaShem called the world good. How did this transition from empty and void to good take place? In the first chapter of Genesis one reads about the Spirit of G-d and light.

Light is clearly a major factor in bringing about this transition; therefore, it should not be a surprise that light will play a major role in the transition from this age to the Millennial Kingdom. Immediately after speaking about the light, Zechariah turns his attention to water:

> "*It shall come about on that day living water shall go forth from Jerusalem; half to the eastern Sea and half to the western Sea; in Summer and in Winter this shall be.*"
> Zechariah 14:8

In a similar fashion to what was recorded in the Ezekiel prophecy, water was flowing from Jerusalem. As a result of this water, called "*living water,*" going forth, another significant change is stated. Whereas there ceased to be a change from day to night, now there ceases to be a change from summer to winter. It is important for the reader to understand what these prophecies are revealing. Not only will there be a new condition for the world as a result of the establishment of the Kingdom; but because of this new condition, which will bring everything under the administration of HaShem, there is no need for any further changes (**until the end of the thousand years**). In other words, when the righteousness of G-d is established as a result of Him ruling (in actuality it will be Messiah Yeshua ruling), this righteousness will continue:

> "*To the increase of the office and for peace; there is no end, upon the throne of David and upon his Kingdom to establish it and nourish it with justice and with righteousness from now and forever. The zeal of the L-rd of Hosts will do this!*"
> Isaiah 9:6 (verse 7 in English)

If one should have any doubt about these things taking place, he only needs to read the following verse to have such thoughts set aside:

"And it will be that HaShem will be King over all the earth on that day, The L-rd will be One and His Name One."

Zechariah 14:9

As was previously discussed, there is an emphasis on the number "one" in regard to the uniqueness of the Millennial Kingdom. Now, based on what is said in the afore- mentioned verse, it is clear that it is G-d Who is the source of all of this transformation. Zechariah continues to reveal changes in the land's topography as Jerusalem is lifted above her surroundings (See Zechariah 14:10). Next, it is stated that Jerusalem will be inhabited. One should understand this as the opposite condition of what all the nations who went up to Jerusalem to make war intended to bring about. It is stated in the book of Revelation and in the Gospels that people will be fleeing from Jerusalem during the end times. However, it is stated that under HaShem's rule there will be no more destruction in the Holy City and Jerusalem will dwell securely (See Zechariah 14:11).

It must be pointed out that this perfection does have one very important requirement; people must demonstrate their "dependence" on G-d. In verse 9, HaShem is called King. Often times, when Judaism speaks about the Messiah, it calls Him King Messiah; emphasizing that it will be the Messiah Who actually will rule over the Millennial Kingdom. It is most significance that Zechariah defines this dependence in light of the Feast of Tabernacles. Each of Israel's festivals relates a different aspect concerning the Kingdom. The Feast of Tabernacles speaks of a "trust" or "dependence" which G-d's people must have in order to find blessing rather than curse.

Messiah's victory will be devastating for all those nations who went up to Jerusalem to make war. This will confirm to the survivors Who is the One true G-d. All the world will learn that He is the G-d of Israel and that Yeshua is the Messiah. During the Millennial Kingdom, one must not only state his faith, but he must demonstrate it as well. This is why Zechariah states,

> "*It shall be that everyone who remains from all the nations which came up to Jerusalem shall go up each year to worship the King, the L-rd of Hosts and to celebrate the Feast of Tabernacles.*"
>
> Zechariah 14:16

The Feast of Tabernacles has a special relationship to the nations. Towards the end of the book of Numbers, in chapters 28 and 29, there is a section dealing with the special sacrifices which are offered during the festivals. One learns from this passage that during the seven days of the Feast of Tabernacles, a total of 70 bulls are offered. Why specifically 70 bulls? Judaism asserts that the 70 bulls relate to the 70 nations that descended from Noah (See Genesis 10 and Succah 55). The Stone edition of the Chumash sites a Midrash that states:

> "*Had the nations realized how much they benefitted from these offerings, they would have sent legions to surround Jerusalem and guard it from attack.*"

With the realization that Messiah Yeshua is King, those Gentiles who remain, will not desire to go up to Jerusalem in order to make war; rather they should gladly want to ascend to Jerusalem for worship and to demonstrate their dependence upon their King, Messiah Yeshua. This is exactly what they are commanded to do once a year during the Feast of Tabernacles. Those who refuse to do so will suffer the consequences of their disobedience. Zechariah states:

> "*And it shall be that if one will not go from the families of the earth to Jerusalem to worship the King, the L-rd of Hosts, not upon them will there be rain.*"
>
> Zechariah 14:17

Rain, in Scripture, is understood as a blessing; hence this passage is teaching that those who refuse to submit to Messiah's rule will find themselves not being blessed. It is important to note that it is not just a matter of not being blessed, for the passage continues and reveals a much greater punishment:

> *"And if the family of Egypt will not go up and will not come, (there will) not be upon them (rain); there shall be the plague which HaShem will smite the Gentiles who will not go up to celebrate the Feast of Tabernacles. This shall be the sin of Egypt, and the sin of the Gentiles who will not go up to celebrate the Feast of Tabernacles."*
> Zechariah 14:18-19

These two verses make it clear that it is not simply the absence of blessings that will be the outcome of ignoring the Feast of Tabernacles, but a much more severe response from the L-rd of Hosts. Although the word *"plague"* appears in this passage, the Hebrew word implies a consuming pestilence which utterly destroys. This idea is demonstrated earlier in this section when the prophet states:

> *"And this shall be the plague which HaShem will smite all the peoples who fought against Jerusalem, his flesh will melt and he stands upon his feet, his eyes will melt in their sockets and his tongue will melt in his mouth."*
> Zechariah 14:12

From this description it would seem that this plague is one of intense heat which utterly consumes the transgressor. When comparing verse 12 with verses 18-19, there is a significant change in the terminology. In verse 12, Zechariah states that HaShem will smite *"all the peoples,"* whereas in the latter passage, only Egypt and the Gentiles are mentioned. This change is most significant. Initially, those who went up to Jerusalem were indeed rebelling against the plan and purposes of G-d; however, this was before the revelation of G-d which occurred at the coming of Messiah and the defeat of those Gentiles who made war against Jerusalem (See Zechariah 14:4).

There is no question that those of the Gentiles who were mercifully spared and survived the coming of Messiah and His initial judgment would **now** have no doubt in the reality of G-d and His power. Therefore, their refusal during the Millennial Kingdom to submit to Messiah and to worship Him and go up to Jerusalem for the Feast of Tabernacles, in order to demonstrate their trust and dependence upon Him, is a blatant rebellion against G-d.

There is another reason why Egypt is mentioned. Egypt is from where the Children of Israel came out as they went up to the Promised Land. Egypt stood firmly against the will of G-d and refused to send Israel forth. Although the English translations usually render the Hebrew as "*Let My people go*" the actual text states "*Send forth My people*". The Hebrew emphasizes a requirement of submissiveness to HaShem's plan, whereas the English misses this and conveys only passivity. Pharaoh only agreed to send the Children of Israel forth because of the Plague of the Firstborn, which brought about death in every Egyptian home. Soon after sending them forth, Pharaoh regretted his decision and pursued after Israel. This fact demonstrates the rebellious nature of Pharaoh, i.e. Egypt, who even after seeing the power of HaShem throughout the 10 plagues, still would not submit to the will of G-d.

Judaism understands that the Exodus from Egypt relates to redemption, therefore Egypt is seen as firmly standing against G-d's redemptive plan 3,500 years ago. So too, during the Millennial Kingdom, Egypt will lead some from the nations in opposition to HaShem's plans and purposes. It has already been stated that there was a change in the language from verse 12 to verses 18-19. The change was from the term "*peoples*" to "*all the Gentiles.*" What is the significance of this change? The term "*peoples*" is a generic word which obviously refers to Gentiles. So why then in the latter verses does the phrase "*all the Gentiles*" replace the term "*peoples?*" The Hebrew word which is usually translated as "*Gentiles*" or "*nations,*" can also refer to those who engage in a lifestyle contrary to the character of G-d. This usage is exactly what Shimon Kefa (Simon Peter) was implying when he stated:

> "*For enough time has passed that we have done the will of the Gentiles walking in lasciviousness, lusts, drunkenness, revelling, partying, and unrestrained idol worship.*"
>
> I Peter 4:3

Zechariah is showing that those who refused to go up to Jerusalem each year in order to celebrate the Feast of Tabernacles are those who prefer the type of actions mentioned by Shimon. Because these individuals are uninterested in the will of G-d, they will ultimately be consumed by His judgment. It is this judgment which will bring about a new reality to the world. The last two verses of Zechariah list several things that will characterize the Millennial Kingdom. The first is in regard to the bells that are upon horses. This section states that it will be written upon these bells the phrase, "HOLY TO THE L-RD". This is the same phrase which was written upon the Head Plate of the priests (See Exodus 28:36). The point is that holiness, which was previously expressed by the priests, will in the Kingdom, even be expressed by horses, which are an unclean animal. Furthermore, it is also stated that the pots in the Temple will be as the basins before the altar. The basins were made of gold and silver and used to cast blood upon the altar. The pots in the Temple were for cooking food for the priests. Hence, the same status that once was reserved for the Temple service, i.e. unto HaShem, now will also be present when feeding the servants of HaShem. Once again, the idea being expressed is an elevation of things to a higher spiritual status in the Kingdom.

This same idea continues to be emphasized in the last verse of Zechariah's prophecy, where one reads about how every pot in Jerusalem and Judah will be "HOLY TO THE L-RD OF HOSTS." When one comes to Jerusalem to make an offering/ sacrifice, he will take from these pots and use them. In other words, the people will also be elevated in status and enjoy the same privileges that were once reserved for the priests. The verse concludes with the phrase that *"there will not be a Canaanite in the Temple of the L-rd on that day."* There are two possible interpretations to this sentence. The word *"Canaanite"* can refer to one who was from the peoples who inhabited the Land of Canaan prior to the Children of Israel entering into it. These individuals waged war against the Children of Israel and were opposed to HaShem's plan for the Children of Israel to inherit this Land. On account of this rebellion, in the Millennial Kingdom, there simply will not be any individuals who are allowed to rebel against the purposes of G-d (until Satan is released after the thousand years). The second interpretation relates to an alternative meaning of the word *"Canaanite."*

This word can also mean a *"merchant."* The idea here is that there will not be any people conducting business in the Temple. This interpretation may have been part of the motivation of Yeshua when He drove the money changers and those who sold animals out from the Temple. When John writes about this cleansing of the Temple, he informs the reader that Yeshua had gone up to Jerusalem because of Passover.

As has been previously stated, Passover is related to redemption. Hence, Yeshua drove out these merchants from the Temple because their actions were against the purpose of redemption, which is worship. In regard to this second interpretation, the fact that there will not be any *"Canaanites"* in the Temple means that in the Kingdom there will not be any who would hinder the worship of the L-rd G-d of Israel.

The final point that stands out in this section is found in the last verse of Zechariah's prophecy. This point has to do with the additional word which is attached to the Torah phrase, "HOLY TO THE L-RD." One reads the phrase, "HOLY TO THE L-RD OF HOSTS" twice. The word "*hosts*" relates to armies. The phrase the "*L-rd of Hosts*" is used frequently by the Prophets to convey to the reader the G-d Who has the ability to carry out His words. Scholars point out that the use of the phrase the "*L-rd of Hosts*" normally is found within the context of a call to repentance in light of His judgment.

Those who would have heard the Prophets relating their words from the "*L-rd of Hosts*" would have understood this term as the most intimidating expression relating to G-d. Not only does the phrase "HOLY TO THE L-RD OF HOSTS" appear twice in Zechariah 14:20-21, but so, too, does the expression, "*on that day*" (a phrase that also relates to judgment). This expression opens up and closes this section. Judaism understands this expression as relating to the final judgment. It also carries an intimidating concept to the reader.

When placing these two phrases together, the reader is forced to conclude that HaShem, Who has the power, i.e. "*the L-rd of Hosts*," will indeed bring His consuming judgment, i.e. "*on that day*," to those who oppose and rebel against the redemptive purposes of HaShem.

Chapter 5

THE PROPHET ISAIAH AND THE KINGDOM

It has already been stated that Yeshua emphasized the Kingdom in His teaching. A good example of this is found in Luke chapter four. In this passage, Yeshua returned to Nazareth and on the Shabbat, He entered into the synagogue. During the worship service, the synagogue attendant gave to Him a scroll of prophecy to read. This fact has great significance. The reading of the weekly prophetic passage is given to one who possesses great respect in the community.

This part of the synagogue service is known as the "haftarah." This word can be translated loosely from the Hebrew as "the summary." Some have preferred the term "the conclusion," because it is read at the end of the service. It is important to realize that whoever receives the honor of reading the haftarah also has the responsibility of teaching the meaning of this passage. The purpose of this teaching was to share with those in the synagogue the connection between the Torah reading that day and this Prophetic passage. In other words, this honor was bestowed upon one who not only the community respected, but one who also had demonstrated a superior understanding of Scripture. The fact that Yeshua was given this honor states volumes about how He was viewed in His hometown.

After Yeshua received the scroll which was from the Prophet Isaiah, He opened to chapter 61. Luke only records that Yeshua read a few sentences from this chapter. It is agreed by all that this chapter is Messianic in nature. This is true on two levels, not only does this chapter reveal information concerning the Messiah, it also speaks in regard to the Messianic Kingdom, i.e. the Millennial Kingdom. The chapter opens with the words:

> *"The Spirit of HaShem is upon Me, because He has anointed Me to proclaim the Gospel to poor ones;* He has sent Me *to declare to captives deliverance; and to blind ones (the) recovering of (their) sight; to send to the ones having been oppressed release; To declare the favourable year of HaShem."*

> Luke 4:18-19

It is important to remember that Luke is taking this quotation from the Greek translation of Isaiah's prophecy (LXX) and it is not exactly as it appears in the Hebrew text. This passage was full of hope for the Jewish people and would have been well known by those who had assembled in the synagogue. The first part of verse 18 clearly speaks to a task being given to one by HaShem. From the perspective of the Hebrew Bible, the Spirit of the L-rd resting upon one was to equip this person for a specific purpose. When Yeshua stated, *"The Spirit of HaShem is upon Me,"* it was clear that He was revealing to those in the synagogue that the passage in question related to Him.

As has already been stated, these verses were understood by all to be Messianic; hence, He was proclaiming to those who would have known Him the best, that He was the hope of Israel, i.e. the Messiah. All the verses which Yeshua read to the people were indeed good news and exactly what all of Israel wanted to see fulfilled. After concluding His reading Yeshua sat down. Luke states that the eyes of all those in the synagogue were fixed upon Him. This would be expected, because after reading from the Scripture it was customary for this one (the reader) to expound upon the passage. Yeshua only said:

"...today (at the present time) has been fulfilled this very Scripture in your ears."

Luke 4:21

I translated Yeshua's statement in a most literal manner, because the words He chose were somewhat particular. Had He stated that this Scripture was about to be fulfilled, it would have summoned the people to take courage, as near was the time for HaShem to move to bring about the outcome of Isaiah's prophecy. It is most significant that Yeshua selected the word Σήμερον, "*today*". Although most translations render the word "*today*", it can as well be translated as, "*now*" or "*at this present time*". The fact that Yeshua used this word and stated further that "*this Scripture is fulfilled...*" (The words that most English translations use to capture the meaning of the Greek πεπλήρωται), is perplexing.

In fact, Luke records in the following verse that the people were confused by these words which proceeded from His mouth. Although in the English most render the Greek word πεπλήρωται in the simple past tense, it is very important for the reader to understand that the word which Luke records is in the perfect passive. This usage has two significant implications.

The first is that the perfect tense refers to an action which actually began in the past, is still happening in the present and extends into the future. In other words, Luke is revealing to his readers that G-d's redemptive work has already begun and continues at the present time (that day in Nazareth), and will extend into the future. The second implication relates to the fact that the word πεπλήρωται is in the passive mood. This means that something or someone must act in order to bring about this redemption. Obviously, the context of this verse would demand that it is Yeshua Who will fulfil this Scripture and establish the Kingdom of G-d.

Not only are the words which Yeshua selected from Isaiah chapter 61 important, but so is the place in which He read them, Nazareth. Although this village was small and insignificant, it is connected in a unique way to the Messiah. Judaism, as well understands this connection, and points this out in another well-known Messianic prophecy. This Messianic prophecy is found in Isaiah chapter 11. This prophecy contains great insight into furthering one's understanding of the Messiah, and therefore warrants a closer examination. The chapter opens up with the words:

"*And a shoot will go forth from the stump of Jesse and a twig from the roots will flourish.*"

Isaiah 11:1

Jesse is, of course, the father of David; hence, the Davidic line or the Messianic lineage is being referred to by this verse. Due to the Babylonian exile, the kings of Judah ceased. At the time of the birth of Yeshua, there had not been a king ruling from Jerusalem for over 500 years. In other words, the Davidic dynasty had been cut down. This concept is seen in this verse by the phrase, "the stump of Jesse." The fact that from the stump of Jesse a shoot will go forth means that although the covenant that HaShem made with David (See II Samuel 7) seemed to be rendered void by the Babylonian Exile, the Messianic promise is actually alive and will be fulfilled.

In the second part of this verse, there is a change in language from the word "*shoot*" to the word "*twig*." The importance of this word is seen in the fact that the Galilean city named Nazareth, where Yeshua grew up, receives its name from the same Hebrew word. It is certainly not a coincidence that this word, which Judaism understands relates to the Messiah, is also associated with Yeshua. As the chapter continues, one learns there is also a connection between the Messiah and the Spirit of the L-rd:

> "*And the Spirit of HaShem will rest upon Him, Spirit of wisdom and understanding, Spirit of counsel and might, Spirit of knowledge and fear of HaShem.*"
>
> Isaiah 11:2

There is no doubt that this verse is revealing the inherent relationship between HaShem and the Messiah. One of the primary ways that Judaism understands G-d is as Judge. The character traits which are being emphasized here are those which are necessary so that a righteous judgment may be executed.

The idea of judgment is significant within a discussion of the Messiah, because the Messiah is King and executing judgment is a primary responsibility of His. In fact, all matters of judgment have been given to Yeshua:

> "*For the Father does not judge anyone, rather all judgment has been given to the Son.*"
>
> John 5:22

In the next verse one learns of the unique way in which the Messiah will be able to discern truth:

> "*And He will smell with the fear of the L-rd and not according to the appearance of His eyes will He judge; nor according to the hearing of His ears will He reprove.*"
>
> Isaiah 11:3

Most English translation renders the first word in the Hebrew text idiomatically. This is a mistake. The idea that Isaiah wants to express is how Messiah's judgment will be based entirely on different means. Whereas in this age, testimony is based upon what one sees with his eyes or hears with his ears; this will not be how Messiah discerns the truth. Messiah will smell and then be able to discern the validity of one's testimony. Everyone is familiar with how a polygraph works. It measures certain changes in one's body, and from the data gathered, the machine is able to measure whether one is telling the truth or not. Messiah will use His sense of smell and will be able to discern whether one is speaking honestly. In one sense, because of the Divinity of Messiah, He knows all things and would not even need to use His keen sense of smell to discern the truth of a given situation. Then why does this verse even appear? Smell is the most discerning of the five senses; hence, what this verse reveals is that during the Millennial Kingdom there will be a heightened scrutiny of testimony. Under the rule of King Messiah, justice will be established on absolute truth.

Unfortunately, in this age, justice oftentimes escapes the courts. A judge may consider evidence which is not accurate and, as a result of this and other inadequacies, justice is perverted. This will not be the case in the Millennium. Under Messiah's rule, one can be assured that Yeshua will administer perfect justice to all.

"*And He will judge in righteousness (those who are) poor, and He will reprove with uprightness (the) humble ones of the land, and He will smite (the) land with the rod of His mouth and with the spirit / breath of His lips will He kill (the) wicked.*"

Isaiah 11:4

The psalmist also speaks about judgment, however in this current age:

> "*The heaven's heaven belongs to HaShem, but the earth He gave to the sons of man.*"
>
> Psalm 115:16

This verse speaks about a separation between the heavens and the earth. Although G-d is omnipresent, the heavens are related to Him in a special way, while the earth has been given over to man. This distinction exists today, but will not exist in the Kingdom. Later in this study, when the book of Revelation will be examined, it will be demonstrated that a primary theme of this book is the special transition that will come about at the end of this age. This transition is simply the establishment of the Kingdom of G-d. The book of Revelation relates this by stating that the throne of G-d, which was in the heavens, is now in Jerusalem. The righteousness that exists in the heavens, and will characterize the Millennial Kingdom, has its origin in Messiah's rule. This is why the next verse states:

> "*And righteousness will be a girdle for His waist and faith a girdle for His loins.*"
>
> Isaiah 11:5

Not only was righteousness mentioned in this verse, but also was faith. Faith is foundational in regard to the plans and purposes of G-d. In fact, the Scripture says, "*Without faith it is impossible to please G-d...*" (See Hebrews 11:6). The intent of this verse is to show that there is a very special relationship between righteousness and faith. In fact, it is faith which leads to righteousness. One of the best places to see this principle is in the man of faith, Abraham. One reads in the Torah:

> "*And he believed in HaShem and it was credited to him as righteousness.*"
>
> Genesis 15:6

The word translated "*believed*" is from the same word as faith. It could have been translated just as well, "*And he had faith in HaShem...*" The close connection between faith and righteousness is seen in the fact that the words "*waist*" and "*loins*" are synonymous with each other. A very important principle in the New Covenant is that it is faith which justifies, i.e. makes righteous. In other words, it will be faith that brings about the Kingdom, which in turn will manifest the righteousness of G-d. It is clear that righteousness certainly does not define the world today. In fact, the Kingdom will be greatly different than the world in which we currently reside. This is what Isaiah expresses in the next four verses:

> "*The wolf will live with the lamb and a tiger with the kid goat will lie down together and a calf and a young lion and a fatling together and a youth leads them. And a cow and a bear will graze together and their young will lie down (together). And a lion as cattle will eat hay. A nursing child will play upon a hole of a cobra and upon a lair of a viper a weaned child will stretched forth his hand. There will not be evil or will there be destruction in all My Holy Mountain, for the earth will be full of the knowledge of HaShem as the waters the sea covers.*"
>
> Isaiah 11:6-9

In this section, there are at least ten phenomenon which are listed as normal occurrences in the Millennial Kingdom. This being the case, it is hard to understand the point of view of Rambam (famous rabbinical commentator from the 12th century) who asserts the following:

> "*Do not think that in the Messianic Age (Millennial Kingdom) anything will cease to function as the norm, or there will be something new in the creation (world). Rather the world will function normally. Concerning what was*

said by Isaiah, 'The wolf will live with the lamb and a tiger with the kid goat will lie down together'; this is allegorical. The intent of the matter is that Israel will dwell in safety with the evil nations who are likened to a wolf and a tiger. It is said, a wolf of the deserts will plunder them and a tiger will watch over their cities, and all of them shall return to the knowledge of the truth and not steal nor destroy; but rather partake of the word in gladness with Israel. It is said (also) a lion as a cow will eat hay. And thus all these things which are mentioned in this passage about the Messianic Age are only allegories. In the age of King Messiah it will be known to all which thing was an allegory and to what the matter hinted.

Mishneh Torah Section Judges,
Halachot Melachim chapter 12

It is significant to note that Rambam's publication, entitled *Mishneh Torah*, is an extensive work of Jewish Law. Approximately 95% of Jewish Law today is based upon Rambam's views. In regard to what Rambam calls the *"Messianic Age,"* i.e. the Millennial Kingdom, it is clear that he and most of the rabbinical world do not take the testimony of the Prophets in a literal manner. Their error is in failing to understand that the way the world operates today is far removed from the original intent of G-d. This failure is also connected to not recognizing the serious consequences that arose from the first sin. The sin of Adam and Eve, by partaking of the fruit from the Tree of the Knowledge of Good and Evil, altered the entire world and that of the condition of man in a most dramatic manner. It was because of this sin that the Torah became necessary to convict man of his sinful nature. In other words, the Torah was **not** part of HaShem's original plan. This is not to say that G-d did not know from eternity past that He would give the Torah to Israel, for HaShem knows all things at all times; but, it was an outcome of faithlessness on the part of Israel. A common adage in Judaism is that the world was created for Israel and the Torah. However, careful study of the Scripture demonstrates that such a statement is incorrect.

First, it needs to be said that G-d is absolutely omniscient; that is, He knows all things and He knew all things from eternity past— nothing takes Him by surprise. However, this perfect knowledge does not mean that all that happens is a direct result from Him. If this were the case, it would mean that HaShem would be the cause of sin, G-d forbid! One must also understand the nature of progressive revelation; that is, that although HaShem knows all things, He reveals them to man over a period of time. In addition to this, it is vital that one realize that Scripture is written in a manner to provide truth to man. In other words, things are written in a manner whereby man is able to comprehend them. In returning to our discussion of the nature of the world, one must understand that how things functioned in the Garden of Eden represented the will of G-d for His creation. It was only because of sin that this plan was altered.

Did HaShem know that Adam and Eve would commit sin in the garden? The answer is, of course, yes. Did HaShem will that they should sin? The answer is absolutely not! Then did this sin undermine the will of G-d and, if so, does not this mean that HaShem is not sovereign? Of course not; however, sadly there are those theologians who hold onto a Biblically flawed view of the sovereignty of G-d. For such theologians, all which takes place in the world is directly related to G-d. One of the outcomes of their errant view is that it eradicates the doctrine of man's free will. It is not the purpose of this book to debate these issues. However, it is necessary to point out that because of man's sin, and G-d's love for His creation, HaShem makes what Judaism calls "Tikunim." The simple meaning of this word is "repairs," but the intent of the Hebrew word involves a much greater significance.

The concept of "Tikun" relates to the redemptive work of

G-d and all of its implications; so that in the end, His will shall be fulfilled in spite of man's sin, the opposition of Satan, and the demonic realm. In other words, HaShem acts in order that in the end, He triumphs and His Kingdom of righteousness and holiness is established. Although HaShem desires that all should repent and receive His work of redemption, unfortunately there will be many who will resist and will be eternally lost. This refusal by those who fail to repent and accept the redemptive work of Messiah Yeshua does not attack G-d's sovereignty, but simply demonstrates that, sadly, there will be those who reject the free gift of faith.

Although the Millennial Kingdom will express the righteousness of G-d and His justice will be executed, it is not the final state for creation. There is, after the Millennium, the establishment of the New Jerusalem. The New Jerusalem is beyond the scope of this book. It is only mentioned here to point out that the Millennial Kingdom, although glorious, does not represent the final condition for G-d's creation. It is for this reason that the Torah and the Temple will be present in the Millennium, but they will not be in the New Jerusalem, as the New Jerusalem represents an entirely new reality. Obviously, it too will be full of G-d's glory and righteousness, but there are clear distinctions between the New Jerusalem and the Millennial Kingdom.

In Isaiah 11 verses 6-9 there are several characteristics recorded that are not present in this age, but these will be the normal condition in the Millennium. The first thing that is expressed is that the enmity that is present between certain species of animals will be removed. This enmity was based in a change in the dietary practices of certain animals. In the Garden of Eden, all animals were herbivorous; however, as a consequence of sin entering into the world, some animals became carnivorous. Today, when one watches a lion feed on an antelope, he naturally sees the suffering of this antelope and is forced to simply acknowledge that this is the way of nature.

Not true! This suffering was not part of HaShem's original plan; but rather it is the outcome of man's sin in the Garden of Eden. This behavior of the animal world, the pain that accompanies such behavior, and ultimately the death that it brings about, are all manifestations of the wages of sin. Although such activity is common and the norm today, it will not be present in the Kingdom. Isaiah states that animals, such as a sheep, which would flee when a wolf is present, will now live peacefully together with it.

In addition to this, there is another interesting occurrence stated by Isaiah. He reveals that a youth will lead them. Why is this piece of information mentioned? In Genesis chapter two, HaShem had all the animals come before Adam to see what he would name them. This is understood as an example of the animals submitting to man. When Isaiah says that a youth will lead them, it shows that it is not because the youth is able to subdue them that they will submit, but it is now the natural condition that animals in the Millennium will exhibit. In other words, there is a return to how things were in the Garden of Eden.

Not only will animals be submissive to man and only be herbivorous in the Kingdom, but they will not pose any threat to even the weakest of mankind. Twice it is mentioned that a young child can be playing around the lair of a dangerous snake and no harm will befall him. Such statements are far from the reality of this present age. The fact that Rambam interprets this section as simply allegories, demonstrates clearly that he misses the connection that Isaiah wanted to make between the Kingdom and what the Torah reveals about the Garden of Eden. The final verse of this passage alludes to Jerusalem, for Isaiah speaks about the Holy Mountain. There is no doubt that Jerusalem has great importance to G-d. This was true during Old Testament times and it is true today and it will be true in the future. There is no question that the following verse relates to the Millennial Kingdom:

"There will not be evil or will there be destruction in all My Holy Mountain, for the earth will be full of the knowledge of HaShem as the waters the sea covers."

Isaiah 11:9

One implication of this verse is the influence that Jerusalem (HaShem's Holy Mountain) will have over the rest of the world. Because Messiah Yeshua is ruling from Jerusalem with righteousness, not only is there no evil or destruction there, but there will not be any evil or destruction in all of creation, for the entire world will know HaShem. The point is that Jerusalem, which has been foundational in G-d's plan during this present age, will also be foundational in the age to come, i.e. the Kingdom. It is hard to understand why so many theologians today, especially those who embrace Reformed Theology, discount the significance of Jerusalem both today and in the future.

In regard to Jerusalem, one reads in the Gospels that the disciples received the Holy Spirit first from Jerusalem, and their witness of the Gospel began first in Jerusalem and then moved to Judah, Shomron (Samaria), and then to the ends of the earth (See Acts 1:8). It is clear that in the age of the Church, Jerusalem was foundational. It is also stated that when Messiah returns, He is returning to Jerusalem and from there He is establishing His Kingdom.

The Apostle Paul warned that in the end times, people would begin to doubt many things related to Messiah's return (See 2 Peter 3:3-4). Likewise, apostasy will be present in the House of G-d (See 2 Thessalonians 2:3). Due to false doctrines creeping into the House of G-d, many will begin to embrace heresy and actually teach things contrary to the Scriptural message concerning the Second Coming of the Messiah. In many theological institutions today, Jerusalem is not seen as holding any spiritual significance whatsoever. A popular minister stated that he saw no greater importance today in regard to Jerusalem than he did for any other major world capital. Can a Biblical case be made for Jerusalem being the place where Yeshua will return and establish His Kingdom? The answer is of course yes!

First, the Prophet Zechariah reveals that G-d (Messiah) will fight against those nations which make war against Jerusalem and His feet will stand on the Mount of Olives, which faces Jerusalem from the East (See Zechariah 14:1-4). The distance from the top of the Mount of Olives to the Temple Mount by foot, is approximately two kilometers. When Yeshua rode into Jerusalem on the donkey prior to His crucifixion in fulfilment of Zechariah 9:9, it foreshadowed an important aspect concerning His Second Coming. Yeshua began what has become known as His Triumphant Entry from the Mount of Olives. He rode upon a donkey to convey humility and to point to the death He would soon suffer. When Yeshua returns at the end of the age, He will arrive at the Mount of Olives and similarly descend, making His way through the eastern gate. However, this time it is not to demonstrate His humility, but as the King of Kings and the L-rd of L-rds. As we have seen in our study of Ezekiel's prophecy, there is a relationship between the eastern gate and the glory of the L-rd (See Ezekiel 44:1-2).

Jewish tradition also calls the Mount of Olives the Mount of Anointing; this is because olive oil was used for anointing oil. There is a play on words here because the Hebrew word "anointing" is from the same root as the word "Messiah." In other words, the Mount of Olives is known as Mount Messiah. It is not a coincidence that when Yeshua spoke for the final time before His ascension, He did so upon the Mount of Olives. The disciples, understanding the connection between this location and the inauguration of the Kingdom, asked Him the following question:

> "...L-rd, are You at this time, restoring the Kingdom to Israel?"

Acts 1:6

After Yeshua responded to their question, it is recorded that He ascended into the heavens in a cloud. It was while they were still gazing into the heavens two men (angels) promised that He would return in the same manner in which He was taken up (Acts 1:7-11). The Hebrew Bible speaks of the Messiah coming in two ways. One has already been discussed, riding upon a donkey. The other is revealed by Daniel, and He states that Messiah is coming in the clouds (See Daniel 7:13). Obviously, Yeshua came the first time upon a donkey and therefore He will return as Daniel reveals. The important thing to remember is that as He ascended from the Mount of Olives, so too will He return in a like manner, that is, in the clouds and also to the same location. The hope of Messiah coming to the Mount of Olives in order to establish His Kingdom is well known in Judaism and is why the most famous cemetery in the world is on the Mount of Olives. It is the return of Messiah to Jerusalem that has significant implications for the Millennial Kingdom.

Returning to Isaiah chapter 11 the Prophet continues saying:

"And it shall come about on that day the root of Jesse, Who stands for a banner of peoples; unto Him nations (Gentiles) will seek. And it shall be that His resting place is glorious."
Isaiah 11:10

Can there be any place more appropriate for the glory of Messiah to rest therein other than Jerusalem, the very place where HaShem placed His Name? It is because of the faithfulness of G-d to keep covenant with Israel that the Gentiles will respond. The very same thing that Isaiah prophesied about the nations coming to Messiah is also stated by Zechariah:

"Shout and be glad oh daughter of Zion for behold I am coming and I will dwell in your midst declares the L-rd.

*And many nations (Gentiles) will be joined to HaShem on
that day and they will be unto Me for a people and I will
dwell in your midst and you will know that the L-rd of Hosts
sent Me to you. And HaShem will inherit Judah His portion
upon the Holy Land and will choose again Jerusalem. Be
silent all flesh before HaShem for I have risen from My Holy
Habitation."*
Zechariah 2:14-17

Zechariah and Isaiah are revealing that Jerusalem, and the
Land of Israel in general, are integral parts of HaShem's plan to
redeem not only Jewish individuals, but also the Gentiles. Some
may counter and say that it is the blood of Yeshua that redeems
and not some piece of land. Of course, I would whole-heartedly
agree with such a statement; however, my point is that when
Israel and the Gentiles see HaShem's faithfulness to His word in
regard to Jerusalem and the Land of Israel, then many will place
their faith in Yeshua and accept His death on the Cross as the
only means of redemption.

There is a difference of opinion among rabbinical scholars
concerning Jewish individuals being gathered up and brought
to the Land of Israel. This debate is whether all Jewish people
are in Israel at the start of the Millennial Kingdom, or if one
of the first things that Messiah does as He begins His reign
will be to gather in the exiles. In regard to the purpose of this
book and the issue at hand, it is not necessary that a position
be taken. What is important is for all to affirm that those who
hinder Jewish people from dwelling in the Land of Israel will
be setting themselves against the work of Messiah. Also in
Zechariah chapter 2, the prophet warns that those Jews who
remain in Babylon (The term Babylon can be used simply to
refer to the exile in a general sense) are commanded to leave. In
order to assist them, HaShem is going to send Messiah against
those who oppose Jewish individuals going to Israel. Zechariah
uses strong language when he says:

> "*For thus said the L-rd of Hosts, after glory He (will) send Me (Messiah) to the Gentiles who afflict you; for the one who touches you, touches the pupil of His (the L-rd) eye.*"
>
> Zechariah 2:12

It is clear that many Gentiles will see what is taking place and respond in faith. When Israel is re-established, and Messiah is ruling from Jerusalem, then those Gentiles who embrace this will be joined to HaShem (of course by means of faith in Messiah Yeshua) and likewise become the people of G-d with Israel (Jewish individuals). Similarly, when the Jewish people see Gentiles worshiping the G-d of Israel, it will impact their faith in their G-d and both Jew and Gentile will grow in their knowledge of Messiah. Three times in this passage Zechariah states that HaShem has sent the Messiah (See verses 12, 13, and 15) and the knowledge of this has great implications.

Isaiah, like Zechariah, focuses on the Messiah. When Isaiah speaks about the root of Jesse (See Isaiah 11:10), it is a clear reference to Yeshua. Likewise, Isaiah presents Yeshua as ruling from Jerusalem and states that this will have a great effect upon the Gentiles. Once again the verse reads:

> "*And it shall come about on that day the root of Jesse, Who stands for a banner of peoples; unto Him nations (Gentiles) will seek. And it shall be that His resting place is glorious.*"
>
> Isaiah 11:10

What is the intent of the phrase, "*Who stands for a banner of peoples*"? The Hebrew word translated "*banner*" can also mean "*miracle.*" Usually this word comes within a context of a victory. The reason why it is translated in this passage from Isaiah as a "*banner*" is that there is a degree of an announcement contained in this word. What Isaiah is intending to reveal is that there is a wonderful announcement in regard to the Messiah, i.e. the Gospel, which the term "*banner*" conveys. This would have been understood by Isaiah's audience. This announcement is that through the Messiah, all peoples can experience a miraculous victory. This same word was also used for the pole that Moses placed the brazen serpent upon in Numbers chapter 21. Also in this context, the idea which is being expressed is deliverance. It is this deliverance and victory that the Gentiles will desire which will cause them to seek Messiah as the text states, "*unto Him nations (Gentiles) will seek,*" The verse concludes with the words, "*And it shall be that His resting place is glorious.*" What does Isaiah intend to reveal with these words? Where will be the glorious resting place of the Messiah? The answer to these two questions is the same, Jerusalem. This is why Zechariah states:

> "*And HaShem will inherit Judah His portion upon the Holy Land and will choose again Jerusalem*".
>
> Zechariah 2:16

As was previously stated, this section of Zechariah is related to the end times; the emphasis on the coming of Messiah is surely evidence of this. It is therefore highly significant that one reads that not only will HaShem inherit Judah, signifying a future significance and purpose for the Land of Israel, but that He will choose again Jerusalem.

The implication of choosing again Jerusalem is universally agreed upon by the Jewish sages as a reference to Messiah ruling from Jerusalem. These words offer strong ammunition against those who incorrectly assert that there is no future significance to Israel or the city of Jerusalem. Perhaps those who teach such errant theology should listen closely to the final verse of Zechariah chapter two:

> "*Be silent all flesh before HaShem for I have risen from My Holy Habitation.*"
>
> Zechariah 2:17

This verse is a warning to all those who oppose the L-rd's plan and purpose for the Jewish people and the Land of Israel, now and in the last days. One should not ignore the fact that in the previous verse the Land of Israel is referred to as "*the Holy Land.*"

In the second half of Isaiah chapter 11, HaShem's promise to gather-in the exiles continues. The language of this section makes it impossible to interpret it as relating to some time in the past. For one reads:

> "*And it shall come about on that day the L-rd will again, a second time, (show) His hand to purchase the remnant of His people who remain in Assyria and Egypt and Pathros and Ethiopia and Elam and Shinar and Hamat and the Islands of the Sea.*"
>
> Isaiah 11:11

Although the list of places are indeed locations where Jewish people had been exiled before and returned, the fact that the verse opens with two references to the future (*And it shall come about on that day the L-rd* **will** *again,* **a second time**) makes it clear that an end time context is demanded. As Isaiah continues, the evidence builds that the final redemption is the subject of this section. The language of deliverance and victory returns as Isaiah proclaims:

> "*And He will lift up a banner to (or for) the Gentiles (Nations) and He will collect the exiles of Israel and dispersed ones of Judah, He will gather up from the four corners of the earth.*"
>
> Isaiah 11:12

There are two facts contained in this verse which clearly place it in the future. The first is that both Israel and Judah are mentioned. After King Solomon, the kingdom of Israel was broken into two kingdoms. The northern kingdom retained the name Israel and the southern kingdom was called Judah. G-d had promised through several of the Prophets that in the last days Messiah will reunite these two kingdoms into one. The second clue that Isaiah is speaking about a time that is yet to be fulfilled is that the exiles "...*will be gathered up from the four corners of the earth.*" Yeshua also spoke about this gathering up in the Olivet Discourse:

> "*And then will appear the sign of the Son of Man in the heaven and then will mourn all the tribes of the earth and they will see the Son of Man coming in the clouds of heaven with power and great glory. And He will send His angels with a great shofar and they will gather together His elect from the four winds of heaven and from one end of heaven unto the ends of them.*"
>
> Matthew 24:30-31

Chapter 11 of Isaiah concludes with a clear promise that HaShem will create the means for the remnant of His people from Assyria to go up to Israel as He did previously from Egypt. It is very important for the reader to understand the intent of the language in this verse. The Exodus from Egypt relates to redemption. The Children of Israel leaving Egypt and entering into the Promised Land is seen in the Scripture as a miraculous act. Although the exiling of the Jewish people from Judah in 589 BC is a great source of despair, there was indeed a returning from Babylon to Judah. However, this is not the case with the Assyrian exile. The fall of Samaria in 721 BC did not have a mass returning to the Land as did the Babylonian captivity. In fact, Jeremiah prophesied that the Babylonian exile would last 70 years before the people would begin to return (See Jeremiah 29:10). This was not the case with the Assyrian exile. There was no clear returning from the countries where those from the northern kingdom were banished. This, however, should not cause one to believe that G-d has forsaken these people. Rather, in the last days their descendants will likewise miraculously be brought to Israel and experience the final redemption that Messiah will recompense His people.

This act of G-d is rooted in His faithfulness to His covenant promises. Obviously this will be a source of great joy. It is this great joy which is the subject of Isaiah chapter 12:

> "And you will say in that day, 'I will give thanks to you O L-rd, for You were angry with me; Your anger is turned away and You have comforted me. Behold G-d is my salvation I will trust and not be afraid, for my strength and song Yah is the L-rd and He has become for me salvation'. And you will draw water with joy from the springs of salvation. And you will say in that day, 'Give thanks to HaShem, call upon His Name, make known among the peoples His deeds, make mention that His Name is exalted. Sing (to) HaShem for He has done great things (this is) known in all the earth. Exalt and shout inhabitant of Zion, for great in your midst is the Holy One of Israel.'"

Isaiah 12:1-6

There are many indicators that this chapter is speaking about the Kingdom. Once again, the familiar expression relating to the judgment of G-d mediated through the Messiah appears, "*in that day.*" The first thing that is revealed about HaShem's judgment is that it is administered with grace, "*for You were angry with me; Your anger is turned away and You have comforted me.*" It is important for the reader to understand the relationship between G-d's anger being turned away and the concept of "*comfort.*" Judaism associates the word "*comfort*" with the Messiah. In the Talmud there is a discussion of possible names for Messiah. These are not necessarily to be understood as His literal name, but words that describe the nature and character of the Messiah. In the Talmud one reads:

"There are those who say, 'Menachem (the Comforter) son of Hezekiah is his name, for it has be stated, for Menachem has put far from me (sorrow), he restores my soul...'"
                                    Talmud Tractate Sanhedrin 98b

Although the verse from Lamentations 1:16 only has the name "Menachem," there was a tradition that Hezekiah was his father's name. Other authorities understand the name Hezekiah as simply referring to the "strength of G-d" (the literal meaning of the name). The idea, which the Talmud is conveying, is that the Messiah will put far from His people grief and sorrow (the context of the passage from Lamentations), and He will restore their soul to G-d. In essence, two very different aspects are being spoken of.

The first is of a physical nature. It is very significant that the verse which is cited is from the book of Lamentations. Sorrow, persecution, and suffering characterized the end of the First Temple period. Prophecy states that these things will also be present at the end of this age. Prophecy also reveals that it is the Messiah Who is associated with the concept of *"comfort,"* which will end the sorrow, persecutions, and suffering of the Jewish people. The association between the word *"comfort"* and the Messiah is so strong that a city was established in the very location that Isaiah promised that the Messiah would begin to be revealed and the city was called *"the village of comfort"* or **Capernaum.** Matthew's Gospel, which emphasizes Yeshua as the One Who fulfills prophecy, presents this as a key indication that Yeshua is the Messiah:

"And leaving Nazareth He came and dwelt in Kfar Nahum (Capernaum) along the sea, between the borders of Zebulon and Naftali, in order that the word through Isaiah the prophet should be fulfilled saying, 'Zebulon and the land of Naftali, by way of the sea, beyond the Jordan—Galilee of the Gentiles; the people who sit in darkness have seen a

*great light and to the ones who sit in the region, even in the
shadow of death, light has sprung up to them."*

Matthew 4:13-16

What is the conclusion which must be drawn from Isaiah's
words in Isaiah chapter 12?

*"And you will say in that day, 'I will give thanks to you
O L-rd, for You were angry with me; Your anger is turned
away and You have comforted me."*

Isaiah 12:1

The answer is that although G-d's anger is appropriate for
His people due to their sin and unbelief, it was the Messiah who
turned away this anger, and by means of His redemptive work,
He will comfort the people. Over and over in the Scriptures
one learns that this comfort is the outcome of redemption.
The major result of redemption is the healing of the effects of
sin and thereby establishing a relationship between HaShem
and His people. It is also significant that the comfort is being
expressed in the next verse with the word *"salvation."* This is
the same Hebrew word from which the name Yeshua (Jesus) is
derived. Another most interesting fact is how this verse relates
"salvation" with HaShem:

*"Behold G-d is my salvation I will trust and not be afraid,
for my strength and song Yah is the L-rd and He has become
for me salvation."*

Isaiah 12:2

Not only is, once again, the idea of redemption (salvation)
being related as a great source of joy, but at the end of the
verse the reader is told that it is HaShem (Yah, the first and
last letters of the sacred Name of G-d, i.e. The L-rd) Who has
become salvation. This is a clear reference to the incarnation,

a major tenet of the Gospel message. Next, salvation is likened to water:

> "*And you will draw water with joy from the springs of salvation.*"
>
> Isaiah 12:3

It has already been seen earlier in this study that water is significantly related to the Millennial Kingdom. The idea of drawing water with joy from the springs of salvation implies that one must go himself to the actual source of salvation, i.e. the Messiah. The salvation experience is characterized with the word "*joy.*" The outcome of such an experience will cause one to want to express, not only his thankfulness, but he will also want to make others aware of the works of Messiah *and* His Nature, for Isaiah states:

> "*Give thanks to HaShem, call upon His Name, make known among the peoples His deeds, make mention that His Name is exalted. Sing (to) HaShem for He has done great things (this is) known in all the earth.*"
>
> Isaiah 12:4-5

The chapter concludes with a very informing declaration:

> "*Exalt and shout inhabitant of Zion, for great in your midst is the Holy One of Israel.*"
>
> Isaiah 12:6

Obviously the Holy One is G-d, i.e. the Messiah. The fact that the term "*Zion*" is used, instead of Jerusalem, reveals that the time period is the Millennium. It is also telling that the L-rd is referenced here by the expression, "*The Holy One of Israel.*" Israel is a significant term and should **not** be ignored nor should an alternate word be used. Sadly, today Anti-Semitism is still present and even growing. Once I was speaking to a missionary who served in an Arab country. He frequently begins his sharing with citizens of that country by using the book of Proverbs. He remarked that the content of Proverbs was very interesting to those he was sharing with, but he did say that there was one great obstacle that he had to overcome. What was this obstacle? The obstacle was the simple fact that the book of Proverbs opens with the words:

"Proverbs of Solomon, the son of David, king of Israel"
Proverbs 1:1

The word Israel represented a problem to this missionary's ability to begin to build a relationship with Arab men for the purpose of teaching them the word of G-d. What was his solution? He simply said to them that the Israel in the book of Proverbs was the ancient Israel and had absolutely no connection nor relationship with the Israel of today. When I pressed him for his theological perspective on Israel's right to the Land, based upon the Biblical covenant, he stated that any covenant in the Bible having to do with land has been nullified and today he preferred the term Palestine when referring to the Promised Land.

The purpose of this book is not to enter into a debate on the theologically incorrect term "Palestine;" however, failure to embrace the term Israel and to understand that the Land of Israel today and the Jewish people in general, still figure greatly and even foundationally to G-d's plan, is an inexcusable error. What would cause one to shy away from the use of the term Israel, when is speaking about the Kingdom, it identifies Yeshua as the Holy One of Israel? The prophet Isaiah frequently alludes to the Millennial Kingdom throughout his prophecy. In the next chapter a review of some of these references will be examined.

Chapter 6

THE PROPHET ISAIAH AND
THE KINGDOM CONTINUED . . .

In many ways, Isaiah's prophecy is the most unique concerning the Kingdom. He covers events throughout different epochs of time and all the while he stays most consistent with his primary theme, namely the G-d of Israel as the Savior. In fact, the name Isaiah is derived from the Hebrew verb "to save." Recently when discussing this matter with another individual, it became clear that, for him, a savior only involved such things as love, mercy, and deliverance. When I pressed the issue further, I learned that his view of G-d as Savior was founded upon a G-d Who did not judge, punish, or have the capacity to be wrathful.

An increasing number of people share this view that Messiah Yeshua will not judge, but eventually will forgive all peoples. To those who hold such a view concerning the Messiah, the question which must be asked is from just what does He redeem His people? Isaiah's prophecy has a great deal of judgment; however in the end, HaShem will establish a Kingdom that is characterized by peace, justice, and righteousness. This

Kingdom is not for all peoples though, only for those who have experienced redemption by means of the Gospel. This chapter will scan the book of Isaiah, locating many of his prophecies concerning the Kingdom. For those who reject this Gospel, eternal judgment shall be the outcome. This chapter is not intended to represent a complete nor systematic overview of these matters, but rather to simply provide for the reader a general understanding of how Isaiah described the rule of Messiah from Jerusalem and what would be the experience of the people.

Scripture reveals that at the present time Messiah resides in the heavens at the right hand of the Father. Satan, who has been banished from the heavens, is present in this age and in the world in which we live. Although this is true, it is also true that the Holy Spirit restrains Satan somewhat. Man must now decide how to live and whether to rely on the word of G-d and find the redemption that is offered by means of the sufficiency of Messiah's work on the Cross. In many ways, it is only the believer who really decides whether he or she is going to submit to HaShem, as the non-believer is in bondage to sin.

This being the case, many believers do not live in the power of the Spirit or walk in obedience to the word. They have a name that identifies them with the Living G-d, but they do not exhibit the behavior that validates His name in their lives.

In the second half of Isaiah chapter three, the Prophet addresses the daughters of Zion. These are women who were invited into the Kingdom and who knew the truth, but sadly, they lived according to the ways of this world. These women, therefore, are more identified with Satan than with the G-d of Israel. Because of their immoral lifestyle, HaShem will expose their sin. It is precisely because of the judgment which the women experienced, that there was a change in these women's spiritual condition. With their sin now exposed and them being shamed publically, they were led to repent. It is clear from this passage that judgment should not be viewed as a negative aspect as some understand it, but a necessary part of HaShem's rule.

It is important for the reader to realize that although salvation is the major theme in Isaiah's prophecy, repentance is absolutely necessary so that salvation can be bestowed. It will be Messiah's return, immediately prior to the Millennial Kingdom, that will bring about a great time of repentance among the Jewish people and those of the Gentiles that remain.

In chapter four, the reader has a glimpse into Kingdom life. There, these same women behave drastically different:

"Seven women will grasp one man on that day saying, 'our bread we will eat and our clothes we will wear; only let your name be called upon us—gather up our shame.'"

Isaiah 4:1

Whereas these women were unmarried and living an immoral life in which they were emphasizing the outward appearance and were uninterested in the role that G-d had given to women; in the Kingdom there will be a significant change. Now the same women are uninterested in the material, even willing to provide for themselves, if only a man will allow them to be under his authority.

Please notice that the number seven appears in this verse (*Seven women*). As previously discussed, the number seven relates to holiness and sanctification; therefore, one should understand the intent of the phrase, *"Seven women will grasp one man on that day..."* as not to mean that a man will have seven wives in the Millennium, but rather women will gladly, and in a sense of urgency, want to enter into the Biblical marital covenant and submit to the purpose for which HaShem created women, which is to assist their husbands to serve the L-rd and to accomplish the will of G-d.

Some might say that this sounds a bit "old fashioned;" however nothing could be further from the truth. The proper implication of the verse is that these women will see the great value and the significance of the marriage covenant from a spiritual perspective. They will also recognize the unique role that G-d has given to man and they will greatly desire to support and help their husbands in fulfilling this role and the call upon his life. It is important to emphasize that this calling is not anything which a man may want to do with his life, but it is the specific plan which G-d has given to him to accomplish.

In other words, when a woman sees her husband embracing and submitting to G-d's plan for his life, then she too will want to submit to this and help her husband in fulfilling G-d's purpose. One of the outcomes of this proper behavior is that the Messiah will be manifested by means of and through the martial covenant. Marriage is a most important instrument that reveals spiritual truth to others. It is not an accident that immediately after speaking about marriage that one reads in the following verse:

"On that day the Sprout of the L-rd (the Messiah) will be for splendor and glory and the fruit of the Land for pride and splendor (a different word appears here for splendor) for the refugees of Israel."

Isaiah 4:2

The term *"Sprout"* is used in a few other Biblical passages (Jeremiah 23:5, 33:15, Zechariah 3:8, and 6:12); where it also refers to the Messiah. The term is connected to the idea that was discussed earlier when studying Isaiah 11:1. It refers to the descendant of David, Who will come forth from the stump of Jesse. An important point alluded to here, and that will be studied later, is that because of Messiah's return and the establishment of His Kingdom, there will be a change in the Land. In the Millennium, the Land that was called a "Land flowing with milk and honey," will return to the renown of its past and even surpass it in its fertility and fruitfulness. Fruitfulness is associated with blessing, and therefore Isaiah is also revealing that the Millennium will be a time of great blessing. Another clue that the context for this chapter is indeed the Kingdom is the reference to the refugees of Israel. These refugees are those Jewish individuals who came out of exile either at the end of the last days of Jacob's Trouble (See Jeremiah 30:7) or in the initial days of the Millennium. In regard to these refugees and, for that matter, all who will be part of the Messiah's Kingdom, Isaiah promises:

> "And the remnant in Zion and the one remaining in Jerusalem will be holy; it will be said to him, (i.e.) all who are inscribed for life in Jerusalem: Since my Master washed the filth of the daughters of Zion, the blood of Jerusalem He will wash (different word than above) from her midst; in a spirit of justice and in a spirit of refinement."
>
> Isaiah 4:3-4

These two verses speak of holiness, justice, and refinement (purity) as key characteristics of the Kingdom life. These things are an outcome of the washing away of the pollution that results from sin. It is also clear that this washing refers to the redemptive work of Messiah. When one receives this washing of sin, it causes the believer to be inscribed in the Book of Life. The concept of redemption continues into the next two verses as well:

> "And HaShem will create over every place on Mount Zion and over those called to her a cloud by day; and smoke and a great shining of a flame of fire by night, for above all is the canopy of glory. And a tabernacle will be for shade by day from destruction and for a refuge, a hiding place from flood and from storm."
>
> Isaiah 4:5-6

The imagery in these two verses should cause the reader to think about the time immediately after the Exodus from Egypt. Remembering that the Exodus is related to redemption, one can also see the protection and the provision of G-d for His people during the Millennium. Although this passage only speaks of Mount Zion, one must remember that Zion is inherently related to the redemptive state of Jerusalem. Judaism understands that the blessings which will characterize Jerusalem during the Millennial Kingdom will also be present and available to all who have experienced a redemptive relationship with Messiah Yeshua, wherever they should reside.

Isaiah's prophecy not only saw the Millennial Kingdom, but at times in his prophecy there are also allusions to the New Jerusalem. <u>Although Isaiah, looking forward, saw both the Millennium and the New Jerusalem and at times did not make a clear distinction between them, John, in the Book of Revelation, revealed that indeed they were two separate dispensations.</u> Beginning in Isaiah chapter 25, the Prophet presents a great feast which will take place during the Millennial Kingdom. Isaiah says that this feast will take place on *"this mountain,"* i.e. Jerusalem (See Isaiah 25:6, 10) and will be for all peoples. The idea here is that all people are invited, but only those who respond in faith to the Gospel will actually be present. It is also stated that HaShem will remove all veils (mourning veils) from all nations. Why will there be no need for the veils of mourning? Isaiah answers this question by stating:

> *"Death (will be) swallowed up forever and the L-rd G-d will wipe away every tear from upon every face and the disgrace of His people He will remove from upon all the Earth, for HaShem has spoken."*
>
> Isaish 25:8

This verse sounds very similar to what is recorded by John:

> *"And He will wipe away every tear from their eyes and the death will not be any longer..."*
>
> Revelation 21:4

Ultimately these things will not be realized until the New Jerusalem comes down from heaven after the conclusion of the Millennial Kingdom. Isaiah combined some of the characteristics of the Millennium with the New Jerusalem because he simply saw these things at a distance and it was not revealed to him all the distinctions concerning these visions. However, John, prophesying more than 800 years later, had revealed to him in greater detail many of these same visions. This is simply a matter of what theologians call progressive revelation. Progressive revelation is when later revelation is built upon that which had been revealed earlier. It should be understood that the later revelation supplements and complements the earlier revelation and is in no way in conflict with it.

It is vital that the reader does not miss a very subtle and underlying truth spoken by Isaiah. Obviously, the removal of tears and death from society are two wonderful blessings that all people would want, but one must understand that these blessings are contingent upon what is said at the end of the verse:

> "...and the disgrace of His people He will remove from upon all the earth, for HaShem has spoken."
>
> Isaiah 25:8

Again, the Scripture links together the blessing of the Kingdom with a transformation that is going to take place with Israel (His people). This is once again clear evidence that HaShem is not finished with the Jewish people or with the Land of Israel. It cannot be over emphasized how important the relationship is between the promises of G-d in regard to the Kingdom and the spiritual condition of Israel.

In Isaiah chapter 26, there is a clear reference to the resurrection:

> "Your dead will live; my corpses will rise up, wake up and shout dwellers in dirt..."
>
> Isaiah 26:19

Judaism understands the coming of Messiah as bringing about a general resurrection, but is this view supported in the Scriptures? The prophet Isaiah emphasizes the concept of salvation more than any other prophet. There is also a clear and strong relationship between resurrection and salvation. In fact, the ultimate outcome of the salvation experience is a new life, which is obviously connected to the idea of resurrection. Biblically speaking however, it is important for the reader to know that resurrection is not tied to Israel in a national sense, as Judaism understands it; but rather to the message that Israel was called to receive and then proclaim to the world, i.e. the Gospel.

Israel was created to bless the nations and this truth is not only related to the fact that the Messiah came forth from Israel, but also it relates to Israel's call to proclaim the redemptive message of Messiah's Gospel. Sadly, Judaism errs in its understanding of the aforementioned passage. For example, famed rabbinical commentator Rabbi Ibn Ezra understood the verse in this manner:

> *"The dead among G-d's righteous people will live and the corpses of my people Israel will rise."*
>   Isaiah 26:19

Judaism has unfortunately developed a highly introspective understanding of the purposes and plans of G-d relating almost exclusively to the Jewish people, and fails to perceive that Israel's greatest achievement should be when Gentiles respond in obedience to the Gospel.

Resurrection and the Kingdom

The resurrection is not a national event for Israel; rather it is one of the outcomes of redemption for those who have faithfully responded to the Gospel. Judaism errs when asserting that the coming of Messiah will trigger the resurrection of every Jewish individual who has died throughout the ages. In actuality, the concept of the resurrection is not specifically outlined or detailed to a great extent in the Hebrew Bible. It is only when a person studies this topic from the perspective of the New Testament, does one receive a more complete understanding of the resurrection.

The first aspect which one needs to understand concerning the resurrection is that the phrase "*The Resurrection*" is misleading. The definite article (the) makes it appear as though there is only one resurrection. This is not the case. Scripture points to four distinct types of resurrections. It is important for there to be a general comprehension of each of these resurrections.

1. **Resurrection (of the soul) after death**: Although the Bible frequently speaks of death as "sleep," it is clear that when one dies he does not enter into a long period of what some have called "soul sleep." The account of Lazarus and the rich man points to a clear consciousness after death (See Luke 16). Not only was there a consciousness, their souls did not remain in their respective tombs.

2. **The Rapture**: There are two primary passages that reveal an event which Paul likens to a resurrection. The first occurs in I Corinthians chapter 15. It is clear that the major theme of this chapter is resurrection. Paul relates to what theologians have called the "rapture" as a mystery. This event involves a change for a certain group of people. This group is not Israel or the Gentiles; rather this group is comprised of both Jews and Gentiles who have received the Gospel message. The event will take place in a twinkling of the eye. The reader is informed that the rapture will be accompanied by the sound of the last trumpet.

This trumpet is likely an allusion to the sounding of the shofar (ram's horn). The shofar has several concepts attached to it, such as repentance, judgment, war, assembling, etc.; however, in this context, the shofar is probably alluding to another motif. The first allusion to the shofar is found in Genesis 22 in the account of the binding of Isaac. The ram which HaShem **provided** as a substitute for Isaac was caught by his horns (the shofar is literally a ram's horn). Abraham called this mountain (The Temple Mount in Jerusalem), **the mountain of provision.** Hence, Paul is linking the **provision** of Messiah's death to the means necessary for taking part in the rapture. The rapture is when the remains of believers, from throughout the ages, are transformed into a new body, a body which is glorious and is eternal. These remains, wherever they may be and in whatever condition which they might be in, will rise and be changed and be united in the sky with the soul, which has been with Messiah in the Kingdom of Heaven. The second passage which relates to the rapture is found in I Thessalonians chapter four. There, once again, those who will take part in the resurrection that leads to eternal blessings are those who are **in Messiah.**

3. **The First Resurrection:** John, in the book of Revelation, reveals that at the inauguration of the Millennial Kingdom, those who died after the Rapture, but who came to faith in Messiah, will live again and be present in the Millennial Kingdom. John specifically calls this the "First Resurrection" (See Revelation 20:4-5).

4. **The Final Resurrection:** This resurrection will take place immediately after the Millennial Kingdom. It will include all those who died prior to the Millennial Kingdom (without faith in Yeshua) and those who died during the Millennial Kingdom (without faith in Yeshua). All those who take part in this resurrection are those whose names were not written in the Lamb's book of life. These individuals

will be cast into the lake of fire and suffer what is
called the Second Death (See Revelation 20:11-15).

It is clear from each of these resurrections that Israel as a
nation or the Jewish people collectively, are not the subject
in some unique or preferred manner to any of these events.
Rather, the concept of resurrection is related to life in the
Kingdom. (This is true of course, except for the resurrection
after the Millennium which leads to the Great White Throne
Judgement). Isaiah defines this life in many different ways
throughout his prophecy. In chapter 32, he writes about the
transformation which the Millennial Kingdom will bring. He
speaks initially about the state of dismay in which the world will
be prior to the Spirit of G-d being poured out at the end of the
age as an outcome of the King's rule (the Messiah):

*"Until a Spirit from on high will be poured out upon us and
the desert will become a vineyard, and the vineyard will be
thought of as a forest. And in the wilderness there will dwell
justice and righteousness, in the vineyard it shall dwell.
An outcome of righteousness will be peace and the work of
righteousness quietness and security forever. My people will
dwell in a peaceful oasis and in secure and tranquil restful
neighbourhoods."*

Isaiah 32:15-18

It is most common to think of the resurrection as only
bringing about a change to humans, but as this verse clearly
reveals, there will also be a transformation to the land, as deserts
will become vineyards and vineyards will become forests. There
will also be social changes as well. Instead of crime and injustice
plaguing our communities, adjectives such as secure, righteous,
peaceful, and tranquil will become the norm. In order to receive
a more in-depth look at the Millennial Kingdom, the twentieth
chapter of the book of Revelation will be studied.

Chapter 7

"THE MILLENNIAL KINGDOM"

(Please note that this chapter originally appeared in a previous book by the same author and has been expanded and revised)

Before delving into the specifics which John reveals about the Millennial Kingdom, let us review a few basic theological points concerning the Millennium. The fact that there are those who deny the Millennial Kingdom is not new. What is somewhat new is the popularity that this perspective is gaining by an increasing number of evangelicals. What lies at the heart of such a theological position? A preconceived and negative view concerning Israel which leads to a theological vantage point that believes G-d has annulled His covenant promises to the Jewish people. For most Amillennialists, Israel is seen as a rebel nation who has broken G-d's covenant and has lost her status **permanently**, as the Chosen People of G-d. However, for those who interpret the Bible more literally, they are compelled by a wealth of prophecy to acknowledge that there is indeed a time in the future when Israel will obey her calling and be used by G-d as the leader of the world. When will Israel fulfill these prophecies and lead the world in worshiping Yeshua?

This time will be at the end of this age and in the thousand years when the Messiah is ruling from the earthly city of Jerusalem. It is the Millennial Kingdom which should be understood as Israel's finest hour. She will finally obey the L-rd and manifest to the nations why G-d has chosen Israel from all the other peoples. In reality, G-d did not choose Israel from among the other nations, but Scripture reveals that G-d created a new people supernaturally, when He opened the womb of Sarah and gave her conception. It is vital for one to remember that, according to the words of Paul, Isaac is the child of promise (Galatians 4:23).

Although ultimately the Abrahamic covenant is fulfilled by Messiah Yeshua, this does not invalidate the fact that a chosen people would come physically from the loins of Abraham and that this people were given specific promises which must be fulfilled. It is the failure to recognize the validity of these prophecies which causes those who reject the reality of a Millennial Kingdom to be forced to interpret the future obedience of Israel symbolically and to ascribe it to Gentile believers. Another unfortunate outcome is the failure to see a literal Kingdom, where Messiah Yeshua will rule from the earthly city of Jerusalem.

Those who deny the Millennial Kingdom (Amillennialists) are forced to do some "theological acrobatics" in their attempt to handle the clear teachings of Scripture, which reveal a Kingdom full of justice and righteousness, having its origin in the earthy Jerusalem. The result for many Replacement theologians (a high percentage of Replacement theologians are Amillenialists) is to assert that the tribulation, which both Yeshua and the Prophets spoke of, is not unique to the last days; rather it has occurred throughout the Church age. Therefore, it is not at Messiah's return when the enemies of G-d are defeated, but rather it is the successful preaching of the Gospel throughout the ages that establishes the kingdom of G-d. It is their belief that Messiah does not return to establish the Kingdom; rather Yeshua takes His place in a Kingdom which has been prepared by the Church. Others combine the Scripture for the Millennial Kingdom and the New Jerusalem together and allow for a period of tribulation at the end of this age, but with Messiah's return, the final Kingdom, i.e. the New Jerusalem, is established. Both views do not see any special relevance or significance for Israel, the Land or the Jewish people, today or in the future. In light of this, Replacement theologians understand that the promise of a re-gathering of Jewish people back to the Land of Israel is actually fulfilled by individuals, regardless of ethnicity, accepting Yeshua in the Land that G-d promised to Abraham:

> "On that day the L-rd made a covenant with Avram saying, 'To your descendants I have given this land from the river of Egypt unto the great river, the Euphrates River."
>
> Genesis 15:18

Replacement theologians teach that it is believers in Yeshua who are the rightful heirs of the Abrahamic covenant and therefore the ultimate heirs of the Kingdom. While this is, of course, true, such a position does not mean that G-d cannot also fulfill His physical covenant promises to Israel in the last days and bring the Jewish people to faith in Yeshua as well. Part of the physical covenant promises to the Jewish people involves the Land of Israel. Please note that the physical covenant promises HaShem made to Israel can have major spiritual implications.

How do those theologians, who deny any future significance to the Land of Israel, handle the numerous places in the Scriptures that ascribe to the Land of Israel a major role in the last days? For them, the Land of Israel is spiritualized and/or seen as an allegory. They equate the Scriptures that grant significance to the Land of Israel in the last days as referring to a spiritual Kingdom and not at all related to the actual Land where the Nation of Israel is located today. This oversimplification of Scripture creates an irreconcilable problem for Replacement theologians. As has been stated several times before, Scripture repeatedly affirms that the way in which G-d will deal *with the Jewish people and the Land of Israel in the last days will be a testimony to* the Gentiles. It is this testimony that will cause many of the Gentiles to come to faith prior to Messiah's return. One of the ways in which HaShem will testify to the Gentiles concerning His faithfulness will be that He will return the Jewish people to their historical homeland.

How do those who do not see any future significance for the Land of Israel explain those verses which address this testimony? They assert that such Scripture is referring to those individuals who currently live in the lands between the two rivers (See Genesis 15:18), coming to faith. For them, this is the proper interpretation for those places in the Bible which attest to G-d returning His people from exile. They reject that the term "exile" is referring to a physical return of the Jewish people to the Land. Rather, they prefer to understand "exile" in a spiritual manner, which relates to one being lost (not saved) and therefore it is primarily the Arab individuals throughout the Middle East coming to faith as the fulfillment of such Scripture.

It is indeed wonderful that there are numerous Arabs who live in the area between the River of Egypt and the Euphrates River who are coming to faith, but how does this testify to His faithfulness to the covenant promises made to the sons of Jacob? One must remember that the Abrahamic covenant passed from Abraham to Isaac, and then from Isaac to Jacob. It is the descendants of Jacob, i.e. the Jewish people, who are clearly the ones whom HaShem will return to the Land as a testimony to the rest of humanity. There is simply no other legitimate interpretation of this promise.

This is but one small example of how numerous prophecies are ignored by Replacement theologians; or how their spiritualization and allegorizing of Scripture rips the various texts from their context. When one examines their explanations for the prophecies concerning Israel, these explanations run back and forth between two positions: either the prophecy had its fulfillment in the days of the prophets, or the prophecy must be applied to the Church. Their methodology is more related to a preconceived bias against the nation of Israel and the Jewish people, rather than in sound exegetical and hermeneutical methodology.

Satan and the Millennial Kingdom

For those theologians who assert that the Church Age (from the ascension of Yeshua to the Second coming) is in fact the Millennial Kingdom, the following two verses, which speak of Satan being bound, offer quite a dilemma:

> "*And he seized the Dragon, the old serpent; which is the Devil and Satan and bound him a thousand years and cast him into the Abyss and shut it. He sealed it in order that he should not deceive the nations any longer, until the thousand years should be complete and afterwards it is necessary to release him a little while.*"
>
> Revelation 20:2-3

Although such theologians understand the Millennium in highly spiritualized and symbolic terms, nevertheless, it is still hard to believe that theologically trained individuals could believe that Satan is actually bound now and has been bound ever since Yeshua's ascension. In their view, it is Messiah's ascension from earth into the heavens which established the Millennial Kingdom. There is a problem with this perspective. It is not His ascension which brings the Kingdom but, according to Scripture, it is His descent from heaven at His return, which will establish the Millennial Kingdom.

For those theologians who reject the Millennial Kingdom altogether (Amillennialists), they have no problem with the fact that at the return of Messiah, Satan is bound and the Kingdom (for these theologians the only Kingdom is the New Jerusalem) is initiated immediately. However, the problem these theologians do have is what to do with the Scripture which says that Satan must be released for a little while (Revelation 20:3). There is absolutely nothing that these theologians can offer as an explanation for this. They cannot provide any exegetical basis for why, after the Kingdom is established and perfection is achieved, that there could be any purpose for Satan being released for a period of time. This is but one of numerous examples of how such theologians are forced to ignore many aspects contained in prophetic passages.

A few Postmillennialists have tried to solve this discrepancy by asserting that perhaps Satan is released immediately prior to Yeshua's return and this forms the basis for the tribulation of which the prophets and the book of Revelation speak. There are a couple of problems with this assertion. First, such a view is in conflict with a major tenet of their theology; namely, that the preaching of the Gospel will be so successful that, in essence, it is the Church that brings about the Kingdom, and Messiah's return is the crowning achievement of the Church's faithfulness. Second, according to the book of Revelation chapter 20, when Satan is released, he does not cause any tribulation at all; rather, he only gathers up those of the nations who want to attack the camp of the saints. In other words, it is impossible to assert that the release of Satan relates to the general tribulation of which the prophets and the rest of the book of Revelation speak. Again, Scripture does not speak about any tribulation which Satan will cause after Messiah's return and the establishing of His Kingdom. Satan only intends to make war, but he is not allowed to do so, and he is immediately cast into the lake of fire.

Although Amillennialists and Postmillennialists have built

theological doctrines which have gathered a large following, they must confess that their views of interpreting Scripture are far from literal. They also leave a great wealth of prophecies untouched, and they attempt to justify doing so by asserting that they are either too symbolic to understand, speak of an earlier period of time, or are fulfilled by believers. For those who believe that one must base his theology upon all of Scripture, the following verse is of the utmost importance:

"*All Scripture is inspired by G-d and is beneficial for doctrine, for reproof, for correction, for admonition in righteousness; in order that complete should be the man of G-d, for every good work having been equipped.*"
II Timothy 3:16-17

The emphasis is that **all Scripture** is beneficial for doctrine. Hence, theological dogma which fails to include in its doctrine the entire revelation of G-d's Holy, Inspired, and Inerrant Word is a theology that should be rejected.

Understanding the Purpose of the Millennial Kingdom

The latter chapters of Ezekiel's prophecy have already been reviewed in this book (See Chapter 3). Now, however, having studied some of the major texts concerning the Millennial Kingdom, one is in a better position to understand why there will be a Millennial Temple. In this section, a brief overview will be provided to assist one in understanding what will take place in this Kingdom. It has already been stated that the Millennium will be Israel's finest hour. This is the case, not because as a Jewish individual this pleases me, rather because the Word of G-d reveals it. It will also be a great time for the Church. Why is this? One needs to remember that part of the Church's responsibility was to provoke Israel to jealousy:

"Therefore I say 'have they stumbled that they should fall?
G-d forbid! Rather by means of their fall, the salvation (has
come) to the Gentiles, to provoke them to jealousy.'"
Romans 11:11

Therefore, the Church will greatly rejoice when she sees
Israel serving the Messiah and leading all the other nations in
obeying the word of G-d. For Isaiah prophesied that:

"And it shall come about in the end of days the mountain of
the house of the L-rd shall be established, chief among the
mountains and lifted up higher than hills and all nations
shall stream unto it and many people will go and they
shall say, 'Come and let us go up to the mountain of the
L-rd, to the house of the G-d of Jacob and He will teach
us from His ways and we shall walk in His paths for from
Zion shall go forth the Torah and the Word of the L-rd from
Jerusalem. And He will judge among nations and reprove
many peoples, and they shall beat their swords into shovels
and their spears into pruning shears, nation will not lift
up against nation a sword and they shall no longer learn
warfare."
Isaiah 2:2-4

These verses were briefly discussed in Chapter two, when we
learned the value of the Torah and that the Torah will have a
primary role in the administration of the Millennial Kingdom. In
addition to the Torah going forth from Zion, these verses reveal
other events which will take place. It is clear that these events
have certainly not taken place as of yet, for they are reserved for
the Millennium. A quick examination of what Isaiah prophesies
in this passage will prove helpful in understanding several of
the foundational points related to the Millennial Kingdom.

First, the mountain of the L-rd must be established. To
which mountain is the text referring? The fact that terms such

as Jerusalem and Zion appear in this passage, it leaves little room for speculation. The house of our G-d is an obvious reference to the Temple, so the mountain is the Temple Mount in Jerusalem. If, in fact, the Millennial Kingdom is here now (since the ascension of Messiah back into the heavens), then the statement which Yeshua makes in Matthew 24, concerning the last days and the occurrence of an increase in warfare, is highly problematic and in conflict with Isaiah's words. For Isaiah's prophecy teaches that nations will destroy their weapons and not learn warfare any more. Here again, if one rejects the Millennial Kingdom, then to what period of time can one apply Isaiah's prophecy? If one is a Postmillennialist, then it is possible to apply it to the period after Messiah's coming. The problem for Postmillennialists is that Yeshua comes after the Millennium and establishes the New Jerusalem. The New Jerusalem will not be administered by the Torah, which of course this passage emphasizes.

To those who state that the Millennial Kingdom and the New Jerusalem are one and the same, other problems are present. First, this passage states that there is a Temple (See Isaiah 2:3), but in the book of Revelation there is a verse which states that the New Jerusalem has no Temple (See Revelation 21:22). This verse states that the L-rd G-d Almighty and the Lamb is its Temple (please note the singular verb "is" is utilized in the Greek, rather than the plural "are," attesting to the unity between the L-rd and Messiah). Naturally, there will be those theologians who will want to spiritualize this passage and say the Temple in the Isaiah passage can be understood as intimacy with G-d and not an actual building. This allegorical interpretation seems to be hard to justify when one reviews the final nine chapters of Ezekiel's prophecy.

In these chapters it is absolutely impossible to reconcile the description of the Temple area, the offerings which will be made at the altar, instructions to the priests and Levites, and the division of the land, with the information provided in the book of Revelation concerning the New Jerusalem. There is simply no exegetical means for asserting that the Millennial Kingdom and the New Jerusalem relate to the same period of time.

The Scriptures do, in fact, provide the Bible student with enough information to rightly understand what will take place in the Millennium and why. First, one is able to identify who will be in the Millennial Kingdom and what will be each person's respective role (according to which group he or she belongs). It has already been stated in chapter one of this book that the Millennial Kingdom will be comprised of the following groups of people:

1. Those who came to faith in the Gospel (**Jewish and Gentile**) prior to the Rapture.

2. Those who came to faith in the Gospel (**Jewish and Gentile**) after the Rapture.

3. Those who are born during the Millennial Kingdom.

In regard to the first group (as we have learned), these individuals will have taken part in the Rapture, have received a new body, and assumed their respective role. This role is to rule and reign with Messiah as Revelation 20:4 clearly states. In other words, believers (prior to the rapture) will have a supervisory role. It is the second and third groups that will make up the citizens of the Millennial Kingdom. A very important aspect of this Kingdom is that Israel will take a leadership role over the nations. This means (as has been stated over and over), Israel will lead the nations in following the Torah commandments during the Millennium. As Isaiah stated,

"*For from Zion shall go forth the Torah and the Word of the L-rd from Jerusalem.*"

Isaiah 2:3

Israel will, in the Millennial Kingdom, finally fulfill the L-rd's purpose for choosing the Jewish people—to be a light to the nations. In other words, it will be in the Millennium that Israel will assume her role to teach and administer the Word of G-d to the entire world. The law of the Millennial Kingdom being the Torah is very problematic for many Christians. Most Christians have been taught that with Messiah's death on the cross the Torah is fulfilled. After all, did not Yeshua say to His disciples:

> *"Do not think that I have come to destroy the Torah and the Prophets; I have not come to destroy, but rather to fulfill."*
> Matthew 5:17

Usually this verse is interpreted to mean that in the past, it was the Torah which was given as a means of salvation, but now it is Yeshua and His death on the cross which provides a new means of redemption. **Although it is absolutely true that Yeshua's death on the cross is the only way that one can be justified**, it is equally **incorrect** to believe that the Torah was given by HaShem as an instrument of salvation. This point has already been discussed in chapter two. There, it was also shown that the Torah has a different purpose altogether. This purpose is to define what is righteous and what defines sin. It is most significant that in the next verse Yeshua states precisely when the Torah will cease to hold significance and no longer have value to the believer:

> *"For truly I say to you, 'until the heaven and the earth pass away, not one yod or tittle shall by any means pass away from the Torah, until all is taken place."*
> Matthew 5:18

The book of Revelation makes it perfectly clear that it is only after the Millennial Kingdom and the Great White Throne Judgment, that heaven and earth will actually pass away and the New Jerusalem will come down from the heavens and from G-d, and will be established:

"And I saw a new heaven and a new earth; for the first heaven and the first earth had passed away and the sea is no longer. And the holy city, the New Jerusalem I saw coming down out of the heaven from G-d, having been prepared as a bride, having been adorned for her husband."

Revelation 21:1-2

Whereas the New Jerusalem will not be administered according to the Torah, in the Millennial Kingdom the Torah will be utilized to teach righteousness to the numerous individuals who will be born during this period. This relates to the original purpose of why G-d gave the Torah to Israel. It was not so that Israel alone would obey it as her own special set of rules; rather that Israel's obedience to these commandments was for the purpose of providing enlightenment to the Gentiles concerning the truths of G-d. They would also come to understand that obedience to these instructions leads to life and blessings, while violating these instructions brings about death and curses. Whereas originally this adherence to the Torah was not mandatory for Gentiles, but would be the result of a Gentile coming to faith in the One True G-d, in the Millennial Kingdom it will be mandated and enforced by the Messiah's rule and supervised by those who took part in the Rapture. It is for this reason the Scriptures inform the reader that when Yeshua returns to establish His Kingdom, He will rule with a rod of iron.

Unfortunately, many believers have **incorrectly** understood Paul's teaching to imply that faith and the Torah are incompatible. Paul never said or implied such a thing. **What he did state is that one is not redeemed by the works of the Law, but only by means of faith, in the all-sufficient work of Messiah Yeshua upon the cross.** In the Millennial Kingdom, one will demonstrate faith in Yeshua by obeying the Word of G-d (Torah commandments). One needs to remember that only those who took part in the Rapture will have a new and perfect body, in which one will not have the ability to sin. This means that both Israel (Jewish individuals that came to faith after the Rapture) and the nations (Gentiles that came to faith after the Rapture) will not have this new body (nor will those born during the Millennial Kingdom) and therefore they will have the capacity to commit sin. When one sins, the Torah contains instructions for the sinner. These instructions involve sacrifices which are offered. These sacrifices kept G-d's punishment away from the sinner. During the Millennial Kingdom, sinners will likewise be required to offer sacrifices in accordance to the Torah, in order to avoid judgment— which would be administered by Messiah Yeshua.

Many believers often protest and assert that such sacrifices are in conflict with the message of the Gospel, which is founded on faith and not works. The Gospel is indeed founded on faith, but the Millennial Kingdom poses an interesting and entirely new situation. Since Messiah's ascension into heaven, believing in Yeshua is an issue of faith. When Yeshua spoke to His disciple Thomas, who refused to exercise faith unless he should see the nail prints in Yeshua's hands and the place where the sword pierced Yeshua's side, Yeshua said to him:

> "Bring your finger here, and see My hands; and bring your hand and cast into My side; and do not be faithless, rather believe."

> John 20:27

Yeshua scolded Thomas for having to see with his eyes in order to believe. Yeshua also stated that those who come to faith because of seeing, are not blessed in the same manner as those who did not see, yet believed (See John 20:29). One needs to remember that in the Millennial Kingdom Yeshua will be physically present. He will be ruling from the Holy of Holies in Jerusalem. For one to ask another, "Do you believe in Yeshua" is, in one sense, a meaningless question because every eye will see

Him (Isaiah 52:8). The one who disobeys Him, i.e. violates the Torah, will meet the discipline of His rod of iron. The question in the Millennium is not, "Do you believe in Yeshua," that is, "Does He exist," or "Is He the L-rd's Anointed?" Why are these questions no longer relevant? The answer is because Yeshua is there; He is the King and His rule is not a matter of debate. Rather, the question is, "Are you going to obey Him?" Faith in the Millennial Kingdom will be displayed through following the framework which the Torah contains.

Obviously, Torah law involves sacrifices, and many understand these sacrifices now to be in conflict with the purposes of G-d, ever since Messiah's death on the Cross. However, this is not the case. These sacrifices do **not** add to Yeshua's work or complete it, for His work was **absolutely sufficient**. Rather, these sacrifices are offered in memorial to Yeshua's death on the cross.

In order for one to appreciate this issue, he must understand the difference between atonement and redemption. Atonement is derived from the Hebrew word which relates to a covering. The best evidence of this is found in HaShem's instructions to Noah:

> "*You (Noah) make an ark of gopher wood (with) quarters you shall make the ark; and you shall* **cover** *it inside and out with a* **covering**."
>
> Genesis 6:14

This same Hebrew root from which the word "*atonement*" is derived is found twice in this verse. The first occurrence clearly shows that its basic meaning is "*to cover*." In regard to the second occurrence, which I translate as a "*covering*," most English translations prefer to render it with either the word "*pitch*" or "*tar*." There is clearly a play on words in the Hebrew text. The same word is repeated, not to emphasize some type of material which had to be used, but rather to emphasize how important and necessary a covering was to the well-being of those in the ark.

One must remember that the context for this passage is G-d's judgment. There is great significance in the fact that the ark needed an "atonement" (covering) in order to provide the deliverance from HaShem's judgment. Once again, atonement only covers the sin temporarily; however, it does not remove the need for punishment. In other words, atonement only provided a delaying of the punishment (judgment) until the final redemption (by means of the Messiah) was offered and hopefully received. The Torah sacrifices, which took place on the altar, always anticipated a superior sacrifice which would bring about redemption.

Redemption is far superior to atonement. Redemption actually expunges sin completely and removes the need for punishment altogether. Redemption should be understood as a payment which causes many outcomes, one of which is that it changes the status of the one who is redeemed from profane (rejected by G-d and an object of His judgment) to Holy (accepted by G-d and set apart for His purposes). It is important that each person develops a proper perspective of the sacrifices which will be offered during the Millennial Kingdom. The sacrifices will be similar in one sense to the sacrifices prior to Yeshua's death, which all pointed to His future redemptive work on the cross. Perhaps an illustration from Hassidic Judaism might assist one in understanding this point.

The deceased Lubavitcher Rebbe, Menachem Mendel Schneerson, taught a very interesting lesson concerning the Old Testament sacrifices. He stated that there is a special quality to the Passover sacrifice. Since Passover is known as the festival of redemption, one should rightly understand the Passover lamb as an offering, which achieved redemption (physical) for the Children of Israel. In other words, by the merit of keeping Passover, the Children were set free from the bondage of slavery in Egypt. **Rabbi Schneerson said that all the sacrifices prior to**

Passover (the first Passover) **pointed to the Passover offering and the redemption it provided, and all the sacrifices thereafter, pointed back to it.**

In a parallel manner, followers of Yeshua should realize that His death on the cross took place on the fourteenth day of the Hebrew month of Nissan (Passover Day). This was not a mere coincidence, but rather it announced the eternal redemption that the Passover lamb in Egypt only symbolized. Most believers have no problem asserting that all the sacrifices prior to Yeshua's death pointed forward to what He would achieve on the cross; therefore, there should not be any difficulty asserting that those sacrifices in the Millennial Kingdom will point back, in memorial to Yeshua's all sufficient sacrifice on the cross.

Again, when the Millennial Kingdom begins, all those residing in it will be believers. This means that in addition to those who took part in the Rapture, there will be Jews and Gentiles alike who came to faith in the second half of the seven year period (after the Abomination of Desolation). It has already been pointed out that those who share in the Rapture receive a new and glorified body. In this new body they will **not** be able to procreate. However, in regard to those who come to faith after the Rapture and during the tribulation period, albeit that they are saved and eternally secure in Messiah, they will not be in a glorified body, and therefore they will be able to procreate.

This fact has some important implications. One is that even though initially all of the residents of the Millennial Kingdom will be believers, there will be people born during the thousand years who will have to make a decision concerning Messiah Yeshua. These individuals will be expected to observe the Torah as the law of the Kingdom and will learn what it means to live in a world under the righteous rule of Messiah Yeshua. But in the end, whether or not they accept Yeshua is a personal decision. It is precisely because of the necessity of those who are born during the Millennium to make a decision concerning Yeshua, that the following piece of information is recorded:

"And when the thousand years should be finished, Satan will be released from his prison and will go forth to deceive the nations…"

Revelation 20:7-8a

Satan's release is in accordance with the purposes of G-d. It is not that he escaped or possessed the power on his own to go forth from the prison where the L-rd had him bound. The sovereignty of G-d is not undermined by Satan's release; rather He provides these individuals with a real choice, namely Yeshua or Satan. It is hard to fathom that after living in the Kingdom of the Messiah that anyone would choose not to surrender to Yeshua and His perfect rule. Yet, as remarkable as it is, there will be many who will choose Satan instead of Yeshua. In examining all of Revelation 20:8 one reads:

"And he shall go forth to deceive the nations, those in the four corners of the earth; Gog and Magog, to assemble them for war— **the number being as the sand of the sea."**

According to this verse, a great number of the very individuals who saw and experienced the righteousness of Yeshua will join with Satan to make war with the saints and attack Jerusalem (See Revelation 20:9). This war will not be accompanied with any period of tribulation like the final seven years. In fact, the clear indication from the Scripture is that this war will be very anticlimactic. In reality, a war does not actually occur. For as the enemies move against the people of G-d and the Holy City of Jerusalem, the reader is not told of a great battle, nor is there any mention of Messiah's coming. It is most informative that one does not read in this account any of the details that are part of the end of the tribulation period. All the reader is told about this *"war"* is that, as the enemy moves to attack, fire will come down from heaven and will consume all those who aligned themselves with Satan.

There are those who assert that the Millennial Kingdom and the Church Age are one and the same (Amillennialists), and when Messiah returns He will establish the New Jerusalem. As the material in Revelation chapter 20 reveals, such a view is impossible to reconcile with the Biblical account concerning the Millennium.

Some point out that in regard to this war the phrase "*Gog and Magog*" appears. Because the Scriptures state that the war of Gog and Magog is the battle of Armageddon, should not one conclude that this war, mentioned in Revelation 20:8-9, is actually the war which concludes the tribulation period? This is not a correct assumption. The purpose of the names "*Gog and Magog*" appearing in this section is not to identify this battle as taking place at the end of the Millennium with the same conflict which Ezekiel speaks of in chapters 38 and 39. John simply uses these names to inform the reader that the same outcome which the war of Gog and Magog produced will be the outcome of those who go up to Jerusalem at the end of the Millennium, namely a resounding defeat. John provides a clue that he is not referring to the literal Gog and Magog in this verse. The reader should notice that the phrase before Gog and Magog are mentioned is "*those in the four corners of the earth.*"

The literal Gog was the leader of the land of Magog, which most scholars identify as being North of Israel. Hence, it makes no sense to speak of the four corners of the earth with Gog and Magog, if one is using these names in a literal manner. John frequently, in the book of Revelation, takes prophetic terms and events which are well known from the T'nach (Old Testament) and alters them in order to assist the reader in comprehending what will occur in the last days. There are other reasons provided in this section (Revelation chapter 20) which make it exegetically impossible to combine the Millennial Kingdom and the New Jerusalem into the same period or assert that the Millennium is actually this present age. For example, after the defeat of those who attempted to attack the saints and the Holy City of Jerusalem, one reads:

> "*And the Devil, the one who deceives them was cast into the lake of fire and sulfur; where the beast and the false prophet are and where they will be tortured day and night forever and ever.*"
>
> Revelation 20:10

Close attention to the Greek grammar reveals that when the Devil is released from his prison, the beast and the false prophet were not. This means that during the battle after the Millennium, the beast and false prophet were bound in the lake of fire and sulfur. It was Satan who acted alone in deceiving the nations and leading them into this battle. However, in the war of Armageddon, it is clearly stated that the beast and the false prophet were present and played a major role.

Another fact which underscores the position that the Millennial Kingdom and the New Jerusalem are **not** the same is the very different description one finds for Jerusalem in the Millennium and for the Eternal New Jerusalem. It is not the objective of this book to discuss the New Jerusalem; however, let it suffice to say for now that the New Jerusalem is described using language very similar to the Garden of Eden, while such imagery is not used for the Millennial Jerusalem.

Isaiah's Final Chapters and the Millennium

Some of what Isaiah stated about the Millennial Kingdom has been previously discussed in this book (See Chapters 5 and 6). In actuality, an entire book could be written about the information which the prophet provides concerning the Millennium. The purpose of this section is to present a brief summary of the final two chapters of Isaiah's prophecy and demonstrate that the events the Prophet describes could only take place in the Millennial Kingdom and not the New Jerusalem.

The first part of chapter 65 is the L-rd's response to Israel's prayer in the previous chapter. In this prayer, there are clear references to the fact that the Land of Israel, including Jerusalem, is in ruins and the Jewish people are suffering greatly. In His response to this prayer, G-d states emphatically that their suffering and the physical condition of the land is all because of Israel's rebellion:

"I have stretched forth My hands all day to a highly disobedient people, who walk in a way which is not good, after their own thoughts."

Isaiah 65:2

The Hebrew word which I translated *"highly disobedient"* also appears in Deuteronomy 21:18. It speaks of a son who is so rebellious and disobedient that his parents will take him to the judges of the city in order for their son to be stoned to death. Therefore, Isaiah is underscoring that the spiritual condition of the Jewish people is indeed the cause for her very difficult physical condition. In spite of Israel's idolatry and numerous other sins, **G-d will not utterly destroy her, nor will He annul His covenant with Israel.**

In fact, HaShem will move in the last days and return the Jewish people to their land. Likewise, the places which were desolate will blossom (See Isaiah 65:8-10). Even though Israel will be reestablished, her suffering will not be over. Why is this? The answer is that although many of the Jewish people will have returned to the Land, there is still a serious spiritual problem.

The majority of the people will still act without faith and behave rebelliously in regard to the word of G-d. Therefore, a time of harsh punishment will befall her. However, this time Israel's suffering will bring about a significant change in the people. They will finally seek G-d and look for the promise of redemption through the Messiah. During the final days of this age, Israel will respond to the L-rd according to His truth:

> "*The one who blesses himself in the land will bless himself in the G-d of Amen, and the one who takes an oath in the land will swear in the G-d of Amen; for the previous troubles will be forgotten, for they are hidden from My eyes.*"
>
> Isaiah 65:16

It is most interesting how G-d is referred to in this verse: "*The G-d of Amen.*" The Hebrew word "*amen*" relates to two important Biblical concepts— faith and truth. It is because Israel will finally respond to the L-rd according to His truth and with faith, that G-d will manifest His promises to her and fulfill the covenant He made with the Patriarchs. In order to bring about this change, HaShem will place His heavy hand of discipline upon His people. This discipline will be experienced by Israel by means of the nations persecuting her.

It will be this harsh discipline that will bring Israel to seek G-d's deliverance according to the revelation of His word. Although the nations play a role in G-d's plan, they will not do so out of obedience. In other words, HaShem simply uses their sinful behavior to bring about a righteous outcome. G-d will not cause these nations to sin, for G-d has no part in sin! This is simply an example of what Paul teaches, "*...all things working together for good...*" (See Romans 8:28).

In the next verse of Isaiah, G-d reveals what His ultimate plan is:

> "*For behold, I am creating a new heavens and a new earth, for the former things will not be remembered and these things will* (no longer) *be upon* (one's) *heart.*"
>
> Isaiah 65:17

The use of the phrase "*new heavens and a new earth*" has caused some to incorrectly associate the events of this section of Isaiah's prophecy with the New Jerusalem, which John describes with similar language in the book of Revelation. John states that it is the outcome of G-d creating a "*new heaven and a new earth*" which brings about the New Jerusalem (Revelation 21:1-2). The error which must be avoided, is to assume that because this same phrase appears here, and also in the book of Revelation, that both Isaiah and John were discussing the same event and therefore the subject of these two passages is the New Jerusalem.

What this passage teaches is that the Millennial Kingdom is a necessary part of the preparation for the New Jerusalem. One must pay close attention to the grammar which is utilized in this verse. The same word which is found in this verse is also found in Genesis 1:1:

"*In the beginning G-d created the heavens and the earth...*"

One should note that the verb which both passages have in common (*create*) is in a different tense in the two verses. In the Genesis text, the verb is in the past tense "*created,*" while in the Isaiah text the verb is in the present tense. Students of the Hebrew Bible know that the use of the present tense is somewhat rare in the T'nach (Old Testament); hence, Isaiah is emphasizing that the creation of a "*new heaven and a new earth*" is in process, but not yet a reality in this chapter of Isaiah. The proof for such an interpretation is found a few verses later in this chapter:

"*It shall not be from there any longer a young child or an old man who will not fulfill his days; for a youth is a hundred years old and the sinner who will die at a hundred years old will be* (considered as) *cursed.*"

Isaiah 65:20

This verse is revealing that during the Millennial Kingdom people will live much longer than they do now. The text states that a hundred-year-old will be considered to be a mere youth and a sinner who has his life ended at a hundred years old will be considered to be highly cursed with a short life.

This is certainly not the situation today, and will **not** be the situation in the New Jerusalem either. When John speaks about the New Jerusalem, he specifically states that there (in the New Jerusalem) there will no longer be death (See Revelation 21:4). Therefore, since Isaiah reveals a time which could **not** be considered today, and is clearly **not** the New Jerusalem, then the only possible solution is that Isaiah must, in fact, be speaking about the Millennial Kingdom.

Again, there is indisputable evidence from Scripture that the period from Messiah's ascension to His Second coming, i.e. today, **should not be considered to be the Millennial Kingdom**. In addition to this, it is clear that the immediate outcome, when Yeshua returns, is not the New Jerusalem. Hence, there is indeed a Millennial Kingdom and those who either assert it is now, or that it is synonymous with the New Jerusalem, are clearly in error.

The final chapter of Isaiah's prophecy (chapter 66) continues to reveal truth about the Millennium. Whereas the New Jerusalem will be the eternal state of peace and perfection, the Millennial Kingdom will have elements of imperfection which will cause Messiah Yeshua to move quickly against such imperfection, rendering His judgment. The purpose of this judgment is to maintain righteousness in His Kingdom. It is clear from this chapter that the Torah is the rule of law for His administration. Evidence for this is that sacrifices were being offered and observances such as Shabbat and the New Moon (Rosh Chodesh) were followed.

In the opening verses of this chapter, HaShem is not pleased with the people's offerings. The reason for this is because those who are making these sacrifices are not doing so with a contrite heart and a broken spirit (See verse 2). They have falsely believed that they could practice whatever evil deeds they desired and gain atonement and find forgiveness by simply offering a sacrifice.

It is important to note that this passage is introduced with the verse which states:

> *"Thus said HaShem, 'The heavens are My throne and the earth is My footstool..."*
>
> Isaiah 66:1

The Millennial Kingdom will be unlike any period before it. Although the glory of G-d had resided in the Temple previously, during the Millennium HaShem will personally reign in this world by means of Messiah Yeshua. Yeshua will know the heart condition of those who offer sacrifices. It is clear that it is the condition of the heart which is much more important than that of the sacrifice itself. Therefore, those who fail to understand the purpose and the significance of the sacrifices and for that matter, all the elements which relate to His rule based upon the Torah, will quickly receive judgment. As the prophet announces:

> *"For behold HaShem with fire will come, and as a tornado with His chariots; to bring about repentance with the heat of His anger and with His rebuke (that will be expressed) in flames of fire. For in fire will be HaShem's judgment, with a sword (He will slay) all flesh and many will be the corpses of the L-rd."*
>
> Isaiah 66:15-16

The next verse provides an example of why HaShem is so angry and His wrath is poured out:

> *"They sanctify and purify themselves (going) to the gardens, one after another; in the midst of eating pork, abominable*

*(meat) and even the mouse. Together they will be brought
to an end, declares the L-rd."*

Isaiah 66:17

This verse speaks about elements of pagan worship. It shows that, in spite of Messiah Yeshua's righteous rule, there will still be those who practice idolatrous behavior in an attempt to *"sanctify and purify themselves."* The word *"gardens"* refers to places of ritualistic pagan worship. Not only are these individuals' actions improper, but so too is their diet. Today, most believers do not give any thought to what they eat, from a spiritual perspective. However, in the Millennial Kingdom every aspect of one's life will be administered according to Torah law. The eating of pork and other meats which are forbidden in the Bible will also be forbidden during the Millennial Kingdom and those who violate such laws will be severely punished. It may seem hard for many believers to accept that Yeshua will enforce the dietary requirements of the Torah. Again, one must remember that in the Millennial Kingdom every aspect of one's existence must reflect the holiness and the righteousness which are revealed and defined by the Torah.

The chapter concludes with a statement emphasizing the fact that Yeshua has perfect knowledge of all things:

"And I (know) their deeds and their thoughts; (the age) has come to gather all the nations and the languages, and they will come and will see My Glory."

Isaiah 66:18

The intent of this verse is not only to reveal that Yeshua knows all, but also that it will be His perfect judgment (righteousness) which will be one of the primary ways in which His glory is manifested.

After speaking about the glory of Messiah being manifested, the following verse relates to Jewish individuals who were in exile, i.e. in nations that were far away from the knowledge of the G-d of Israel. It will be those Jewish individuals who:

"...will declare My glory among the Gentiles."

Isaiah 66:19

In the next verse one reads:

"And they will bring all their brethren from those nations (with) an offering to HaShem...to My holy mountain, Jerusalem, said HaShem, just as the Children of Israel brought the offering in a pure vessel (to) the Temple of HaShem."

Isaiah 66:20

Then Isaiah informs the reader that from the Gentiles (or Nations), there will be taken men to serve as priests and Levites:

"And also from them I will take for priests and for Levites said HaShem."

Isaiah 66:21

There is a debate concerning this verse, as to who is the direct object of the sentence. Some Christian scholars understand the word *"them"* as in *"And also from them,"* referring to Gentiles (non-Jews). It is important to note that the Hebrew word סיים can be understood as *"Gentiles"* or it can refer to *"Nations,"* as in countries. The Christian scholars who interpret the verse to mean that HaShem will make priests and Levites from Gentiles, base this interpretation upon the understanding of the phrase *"And also from them"* meaning Gentiles, rather than paying close attention to the fact that the direct object actually relates to Jewish individuals. In verse 20, the subject of the direct object was stated to be *"...all your brethren from among the Gentiles (Nations),"* i.e. Jewish individuals. Likewise, at the end of the verse, the *"Children of Israel"* are mentioned and become the subject of the phrase in question—*"And also from them."* Finally, in verse 22, the best proof is found for understanding that this passage is indeed referring to Jewish individuals coming out of exile, i.e. out of the nations or from among the Gentiles:

> *"For just as there are a new heavens and a new earth, I will make (them) endure before Me declares HaShem, thus your seed and your name will endure."*
>
> Isaiah 66:22

Isaiah wants to reveal that in the same way that one can trust in the promise of HaShem establishing the Kingdom, so too can one be assured that He will likewise keep His covenant with Israel. If the correct interpretation was Gentiles being made to serve as priests and Levites, then this verse, which emphasizes the *"seed,"* would be emptied of its significance.

Again, when the nations (Gentiles) see His faithfulness to Israel, they too will join in worshiping the G-d of Israel and His Messiah within the parameters of the Torah. This is seen in the next verse:

> *"And it shall be each and every month (Rosh Chodesh, the Jewish celebration of the new month, See Numbers 28) and on each and every Shabbat, **all flesh** will come to bow down (worship) before Me said HaShem."*
>
> Isaiah 66:23

Please notice that there is an emphasis on the phrase, *"all flesh will come to bow down (worship) before Me said HaShem."* This reveals a fulfillment of HaShem's plan that Israel would lead the Gentiles to worship Him. No longer are Jerusalem and the Temple places of worship for only the Jewish people, but they finally become a place of worship for all peoples as Isaiah prophesied earlier:

*"Do not let the Gentile, who has joined himself to HaShem, speak saying, the L-rd will certainly make a distinction concerning me from His people or let the eunuch say, behold I am a dry tree. For thus said HaShem to the eunuchs who shall keep My Sabbaths and shall choose that in which I delight and hold fast to My covenant. I will give to them in My House (Temple) and within My walls (within the Holy City of Jerusalem) a better reputation than (the physical) sons and daughters, an eternal name I will give to him which cannot be cut off. And the Gentiles who have joined themselves to HaShem to serve Him and for the love of the name of the L-rd, to be unto Him servants, all who keep the Sabbath and do not profane it, and holding fast to My covenant. I will bring them to My Holy Mountain and I will make them to be glad in My House of Prayer; their elevation offerings and sacrifices will be favorable upon My altar, for My House (Temple) will be called **a House of Prayer for all peoples**, declares the L-rd G-d Who gathers the exiles of Israel again, I will gather him to those who have been gathered."*

Isaiah 56:3-8

This passage is strong and clear concerning some of the major principles related to the establishment of the Millennial Kingdom. It is important to understand how these principles work together and reveal HaShem's program for His creation. Perhaps learning the meaning of a Hebrew word will assist one in receiving these principles and the purpose each one of them plays in fulfilling HaShem's will. The Hebrew word is תילכת. There are two primary definitions for this word. The first is *"end"* and the second is *"aim"* or *"goal."*. The idea here is that G-d has a specific aim or purpose in bringing His creation to its final state of being (to its end). Although the Millennial Kingdom is not this final state of things (the New Jerusalem is), it assists one in understanding the character of the New Jerusalem and is a necessary step in moving to the New Jerusalem.

In returning to the passage from Isaiah chapter 56, there are three distinct principles which are stated in these verses. The **first** is that Gentiles are a central part of G-d's plan. Biblically, one knows that a major element of the Abrahamic Covenant was to create a people from the loins of Abraham for the purpose of blessing the Gentiles. Naturally, Yeshua and the salvation that He offers is the greatest outcome of the Abrahamic Covenant. However, Israel was created by G-d to be more than just the people from whom the Messiah would originate (in a physical sense only). The blessings that will characterize the Kingdom, and be the source of a great joy, will, in fact, be mediated to the world by Israel. **Second**, the Torah lifestyle that was given to Israel will also be received by the Gentiles who will, by means of faith, have embraced the Shabbat and hold fast to the covenant. They will also be offering sacrifices. The observance of the Sabbath, the offering of sacrifices, and the mention of the covenant, are all foundational to the Torah. In the Millennial Kingdom there is only one set of laws, the Torah. which will be the standard of conduct for all peoples, Jew and Gentile alike.

The **third** principle is worship. Isaiah provides several references in this passage that relate to worship. The worship of G-d was primary for the creation of man and therefore it should not be surprising that worship will be the major activity in the Millennial Kingdom. Isaiah concludes this section by restating a familiar prophetic truth, "... *declares the L-rd G-d Who gathers the exiles of Israel again....*" Once again, the prophet cannot help to proclaim that HaShem will maintain His covenantal promises to the Jewish people and return them to the Promised Land. Why this repeated emphasis? The answer is to make sure that Gentiles learn that the Kingdom promises are dependent upon the Jewish people returning to the Land of Israel. After the Millennial Kingdom and the destruction of Satan and those who were joined to him, there is a final judgment. We will now take a brief look at this Judgment.

The Great White Throne Judgment

John states that immediately after the Millennial Kingdom, an event will take place prior to G-d creating the New Jerusalem. This event is normally referred to as the "Great White Throne Judgment." A key clue which assists the reader in understanding the uniqueness of this judgment, and who will be part of this judgment, is the term resurrection. The book of Revelation speaks about two primary resurrections. The first resurrection has an entirely different theme than that of the second resurrection. Those who are part of the first resurrection are said to be blessed and holy:

> *"Blessed and holy are the ones who have a part in the first resurrection; upon these the second death has no power, they will be priests of G-d and of the Messiah and will rule with Him a thousand years."*
>
> Revelation 20:6

Those who are in the second resurrection will find everlasting death. The first resurrection includes all believers throughout all the various ages, while the second resurrection includes all who died without faith in Messiah Yeshua throughout all the various ages. This means that all those who rejected the Gospel throughout history, including those in the Millennial Kingdom, will take part in this second resurrection. Once again, for those who assert that since Messiah's ascension the Millennium has begun, a difficult problem presents itself. Clearly the Rapture is one of the stages of the first resurrection. Because it is clear that the Rapture has not yet occurred, but that the first resurrection is complete prior to the Millennial Kingdom, one may not assert that believers are living in the Millennium today. Such an assertion is without a Scriptural foundation.

It is clear that **all** who appear before the Great White Throne will be judged according to their deeds and therefore will be found insufficient to enter the New Jerusalem. The only ones who are granted the privilege to share eternity with G-d and the Lamb are those who have had their names written in the Lamb's *Book of Life*. This is an outcome which is solely the result of the redemptive work of Yeshua on the cross and was bestowed freely only upon all who receive the Gospel. **All** who appear before the Great White Throne will find themselves being cast into the lake of fire and sulfur. It is this act which the Bible calls the "Second Death" (See Revelation 20:11-15).

Chapter 8

THE MILLENNIAL KINGDOM AND THE BOOK OF PSALMS

B oth Christian and rabbinical scholars acknowledge that there is a type of Psalm known as Messianic. Not only do these Psalms provide material about the Person and Work of the Messiah, but one also can learn a great deal of truth concerning the Millennial Kingdom. Only a few Psalms will be considered in this chapter. Therefore, by no means is this chapter intended to be a comprehensive look at all the information which the Psalms contain concerning the Kingdom. Rather, only a brief sampling of the primary Psalms which deal with the Millennial Kingdom will be examined in this section.

Psalm 24

"By David, a Psalm. To HaShem is the earth and its fullness; the world and the inhabitants of it. For He, upon the seas founded it, upon the rivers established it. Who will ascend on the mountain of the L-rd, and who will stand in His holy

place? (Those who have) clean hands and a pure heart, who do not take (an oath) in vain (before) My soul, or swear in deceptiveness. He will take up a blessing from HaShem and righteousness from the G-d of his salvation. This is the generation that demands Him, seekers of His face (presence) O Jacob, Selah! Lift up O gates your heads, and be lifted up O eternal doors and the King of Glory will enter. Who is the King of Glory? HaShem is powerful and mighty, HaShem is mighty in war. Lift up O gates your heads, and be lifted up O eternal doors and the King of Glory will enter. Who is this One, the King of Glory? The L-rd of Hosts He is the King of Glory."

This Psalm is a typical example of Hebrew poetry. The primary characteristic of Hebrew poetry is parallelism. For example, in the first verse the word "*earth*" is parallel to the word "*world*." Each of the ten verses of this Psalm demonstrates this same type of parallelism. It is very significant that the earth is mentioned, but not the heavens. This particular Psalm is one of the enthronement Psalms which were written to be used when a new king took the throne. Ultimately, these enthronement Psalms were composed for when the Messiah would establish His throne in Jerusalem. This was understood as the rule of G-d being transferred from the heavens to earth. Hence, the heavens were not referred to in this Psalm. The primary theme in verse one is the sovereignty of G-d.

Verse two speaks of how HaShem established the world upon water. The idea here is that once something is placed on water it usually sinks. However, the earth was founded upon water and did not sink because it is held, so to speak, by HaShem. Rabbinical scholars point out that in the same way that G-d maintains this world He will, as well, establish and maintain the Kingdom, i.e. according to His providence. Whereas in verse one the sovereignty of G-d is emphasized, in verse two G-d as the Creator is the main motif.

Because HaShem is sovereign, and due to the fact that He created and maintains the world supernaturally, man should worship Him. The concept of worship is introduced in verse three when the Temple Mount is mentioned. Man wanting to worship G-d is good but poses a serious problem. Not just anyone can approach the Holy G-d and worship Him. This is why the following question is posed in this verse:

"Who will ascend on the mountain of the L-rd, and who will stand in His holy place?"

Psalm 24:3

The answer that is provided in this Psalm is most restrictive, as only those who have *"clean hands and a pure heart"* are permitted to do so. The first part of this phrase refers to those who have not sinned in deed, while the second part relates to those who have not sinned in thought. Such an answer, of course, eliminates all of humanity. There is, however, one hope for man and that is the Good News concerning redemption, i.e. the Gospel. The Gospel demands a response. One might understand this response as a confession or an oath. This is why the second half of the verse states, *"who do not take (an oath) in vain (before) My soul, or swear in deceptiveness."* Those who sincerely receive the Gospel are redeemed and are blessed with salvation. This truth is clearly affirmed in the next verse:

"He will take up a blessing from HaShem and righteousness from the G-d of his salvation."

Psalm 24:5

In other words, the outcome of one accepting (confessing) the Gospel is that He will receive a blessing. The primary aspect of this blessing is that the sinner is imparted with the very righteousness of HaShem which is a direct result of salvation. It is significant that when HaShem is referred to in this verse He is called "*the G-d of his salvation.*"

In the next verse, a time (epoch) is spoken of when Jacob (the Jewish people) will seek the L-rd. Once again, the Bible clearly reveals that prior to the Messiah returning to earth to establish His Kingdom, Israel needs to go through a spiritual change whereby the Jewish people will turn and seek the Messiah. What will cause this change? The answer is intense persecution and tribulation. This fact will be addressed by the Psalmist in verses eight and ten, but what immediately is revealed is the outcome of Israel's spiritual change. In verses seven and nine the same sentence appears:

> "*Lift up O gates your heads, and be lifted up O eternal doors and the King of Glory will enter.*"
>
> Psalm 24:7, 9

These verses are clearly a call to Jerusalem to make the necessary preparations and response to the coming of the Messiah. In this Psalm, Messiah Yeshua is called "*The King of Glory.*" In verse eight there is a problematic statement for those who deny the deity of Yeshua. Although there is strong consensus that the subject of the enthronement Psalms is the Messiah, it is actually HaShem Who is referenced. He is called "*powerful and mighty in war.*" Why is war introduced into the text?

As previously mentioned, it will be intense persecution and tribulation which will cause Israel to repent and to seek deliverance from her enemies. Who is it that is promised to save and to redeem Israel in the last days? Obviously the Messiah, for He will return and deliver the Jewish people from all the nations who will be attacking her. Therefore, it should not be a surprise that the Messiah is called "*mighty in war.*" In the final verse Messiah is called "*The L-rd of Hosts.*" Of course the term "*Hosts*" is derived from the Hebrew word for armies.

Hence, there is another reference to the Messiah coming to

wage war with the enemies of Israel in the last days. The last word of the Hebrew text is "*Selah.*" This word appears twice in the Psalm, in verses six and ten. It is most significant that it appears after the word "*Jacob*" and after the phrase "*The King of Glory.*" What is the purpose in the fact that only after these two places, does this word appear? The purpose is to show the close relationship between Israel and the Messiah. Some Hebrew scholars understand the meaning of this word, which is usually not translated, as "*forever.*" Hence, the message which is being conveyed here is that the relationship between Israel and HaShem is unbreakable.

Psalm 30

"*A Psalm. A song for the dedication of the Temple. By David. I will exalt You O L-rd, for you have drawn me up, and my enemies have not rejoiced over me. The L-rd my G-d I have cried out unto You and You have healed me. O L-rd You have lifted from Sheol my soul, You kept me alive from my decent into the pit. Sing to HaShem O Chassidim and give thanks to the mention of His holiness. For a moment is His anger, life is His delight. In the evening one lies down with weeping, but in the morning (there are) shouts of joy. And I have said in my tranquility I will not stumble. O L-rd, in your delight You have established my strong defense (literally, my strong mountain); You have hid Your face and I was afraid. Unto You O L-rd I have cried and to my Master I have sought grace. What profit is in my blood (death), in my decent to destruction; does dirt give thanks to You, does it declare Your truth? Hear O L-rd and be gracious to me, O L-rd be my Helper. You have turned my lament into dancing for me, You have opened my sackcloth and You have girded me with gladness. On account of this (my) honor will sing to you and it will not cease O L-rd my G-d. I will give thanks to You forever.*"

Psalm 30 is called *"a song for the dedication of the Temple."*
It was written by King David. The question that must be asked
is which Temple is being referred to by David in this Psalm? In
verses 2-4, there are four clear references to the resurrection.
This fact should cause one to conclude that the Temple which
David was referring to was indeed the Millennial Temple. There
are but four points that need to be made concerning this Psalm
for the purposes of our study of the Millennial Kingdom. The
first has already been stated – namely, the importance of the
resurrection in providing the context for this Psalm.

Not only is the resurrection related to the Kingdom, but it
also points to the concept of victory. This concept is found at
the end of verse two with the phrase, *"and my enemies have not
rejoiced over me."* The idea here is that HaShem has not allowed
the enemies to rejoice over Israel. Why? The answer is because
He defeated them. Literally, it is David whose enemies have not
rejoiced over him, but because David is the King of Israel and
responsible for the people, his victory is Israel's victory.

The second point is that the recipients of this victory, and
those who will be in the Kingdom, are called "Chassidim." The
Hebrew root from which this word is derived means "grace" or
"G-d's loving Kindness." Hence, one will not experience victory
or be allowed into the Kingdom by one's own merit. Rather,
these blessings are a direct result of G-d's grace. The fact that
the word is in the plural also points, not to David alone, but the
nation as a whole.

The third point is that those who will receive this victory
and who will be part of the Kingdom understand that there is a
very specific purpose in receiving these blessings. David refers
to these purposes when he writes:

> *"What profit is in my blood (death), in my decent to
> destruction; does dirt give thanks to You, does it declare
> Your truth?"*

> Psalm 30:10

It is important for each person to understand that the reason why HaShem created humanity was so all people could praise Him. It is not surprising that the nations have failed in this objective, for so too has Israel.

It was Israel who was called to be a light to the nations, in other words, to teach the nations how to praise G-d and give thanks to Him. It will be in the Millennial Kingdom that Israel will finally fulfill her calling and influence the nations to join her in worshiping the G-d of Israel.

The fourth point is the great transformation which will take place in Israel in the last days and will characterize Israel during the Millennium. This transformation is seen in the last two verses of the Psalm:

"You have turned my lament into dancing for me, You have opened my sackcloth and You have girded me with gladness. On account of this (my) honor will sing to you and it will not cease O L-rd my G-d. I will give thanks to You forever."
Psalm 30:12-13

Initially, the idea of lamenting is discussed in verse twelve. The Hebrew word in this verse for lamenting relates to death, i.e. the outcome of sin. The proper response to sin is repentance. This concept is seen in the term sackcloth, which appears in the middle of the same verse. One reads that HaShem has opened the sackcloth and has clothed the individual with gladness.

In essence, what this verse presents to the reader is the process that Israel will go through in the last days which will conclude with the establishment of the Kingdom. This lamenting parallels a time of persecution and intense suffering that Israel will pass through. This will lead Israel to repent and seek HaShem. It is exactly when Israel is seeking G-d and His deliverance that the Messiah will appear and answer Israel's requests for grace and help:

"Hear O L-rd and be gracious to me, O L-rd be my Helper."
                                                    Psalm 30:11

Some rabbinical scholars believe that David wrote this Psalm for a specific purpose. This purpose was so that when David returns at the time of Messiah's return, he can lead Israel and the nations in reciting it as Messiah takes His throne in Jerusalem.

Psalm 47

"To the leader, by the sons of Korach a Psalm. All the peoples clap hands; shout to G-d with a voice of triumph. For HaShem is Most High and Awesome, the Great King over all the earth. He will speak peoples under us, and nations under our feet. He will choose for us our inheritance— the pride of Jacob whom He loves, Selah. G-d has gone up (on to His throne) with the shout, HaShem, with the sound of the Shofar. Sing to G-d sing, sing to our King sing. For (He is) King over all the earth, to G-d sing a Psalm of understanding. G-d rules over all the nations, G-d sits upon His holy throne. (The) nobles men of the people are gathered, the people of the G-d of Abraham; for to G-d are the shields of the earth, He is greatly exalted."

Throughout this Psalm the idea that is being conveyed is that HaShem reigns over all the earth. In other words, from the perspective of this Psalm, the Kingdom has indeed been established. It is very important for the reader to see one of the main characteristics of the Kingdom. This characteristic is found in verse four:

"He will speak peoples under us, and nations under our feet. He will choose for us our inheritance—the pride of Jacob whom He loves, Selah.
                                                    Psalm 47:4-5

When one reviews most of history, he finds that Israel has been greatly afflicted by the nations. This however, will not be the case during the Millennium. Verse four uses the language of creation, namely that G-d will simply **speak** this change into being, as He spoke during the six days of creation. Obviously, the peoples and nations being referred to in this verse are the Gentiles, and the use of the first person plural refers to Israel. It is important to remember that the Gentiles who are being addressed in this Psalm are the remnant which survived attacking Jerusalem in the last days. This remnant was brought to faith when they saw that it was Yeshua Who was fighting on behalf of Israel. Please note that those Jews and Gentiles who took part in the Rapture (those who are the body of Messiah, i.e. the congregation of the redeemed) are not included in this Psalm, other than they too will be praising and worshiping Him in the Kingdom.

When one reads that HaShem *"will speak peoples under us and nations under our feet,"* it once again reveals that Israel will have a leadership position in the Kingdom. There is simply no way to deny the uniqueness of the Jewish people in regard to G-d's Kingdom purposes. The fact that this truth is repeated so frequently in the Scriptures makes it hard to understand why so many theologians miss it. To simply apply these numerous verses to the Church fails to meet the Biblical definition of the Church being comprised of individuals from very every nation, tribe, people, and language. Furthermore, if the Church is the subject of verses four and five, then what is the reason for the use of the phrase, *"the pride of Jacob"*? The Hebrew word translated *"pride"* does not mean pride in a haughty or self-centered manner. The Hebrew word גאון can mean *"majesty."* The Temple is also called by this same term and the idea here is that it is G-d Who is taking pride or pleasure in the Temple. Therefore, this phrase is actually referring to Jacob, i.e. the Jewish people, as those in whom HaShem takes pride or those who manifest His majesty.

A very important time for the Jewish community is Friday evening. For this is when the Sabbath day is welcomed. According to the Jewish sages, there is a theological connection between the Sabbath and the Kingdom. The New Testament also contains passages which hint to this connection. It is therefore not surprising that the Kabalat Shabbat service (the service in Judaism that begins Sabbath observance) contains several Psalms which are related to the Kingdom, one of which is Psalm 98:

Psalm 98

> "*A Psalm. Sing to HaShem a new song, for He has done wonders; His Right Hand and His Holy Arm have brought salvation to Him. HaShem has made known His salvation before the eyes of the nations, He has revealed His righteousness. Remember His grace and His faithfulness to the House of Israel; See O all the ends of the earth the salvation of our G-d. Shout to HaShem all the earth, break forth and shout and sing. Sing to HaShem with a harp, with a harp and the sound of a song. With trumpets and the sound of the Shofar; shout before the King—HaShem! The sea will roar and its fullness, the world and the inhabitants in it. The rivers will clap together, the mountains will shout for joy. Before HaShem, for He has come to judge the earth, He will judge the world in righteousness and peoples with uprightness.*"

This Psalm, like most of the Psalms which relate to the Kingdom, has an abundant amount of Praise. While it is, of course, appropriate to praise the L-rd for Who He is, this Psalm emphasizes the marvelous things He has done. While some Psalms review the great works of G-d throughout Israel's history, this Psalm focuses upon two specific thoughts. The first is salvation and the second is the transformation of this fallen world into the Kingdom of G-d. The catalyst for both of these is Messiah Yeshua.

Messiah is described first as *"His Right Hand."* In Jewish literature, the right hand expresses the idea of integrity and power. The word *"hand"* can also convey that of a deed or the result of work being completed. It is clear from the text that it is not going to be the successful actions of the Church which establishes the Kingdom, as Post-millennialists assert, but it is the result of the work of Messiah, which was done through His power and integrity. Next, Messiah is spoken of as *"His Holy Arm."* The word *"arm"* is related to the Hebrew root for a descendant or an offspring. It can also express the idea of a sacrifice or offering. For example, the Passover sacrifice is identified by the same Hebrew word עורז. Therefore, when one speaks about *"His Holy Arm,"* what should be understood is **"His (G-d's) Holy Son who became the sacrifice of redemption (Passover)"** for humanity.

Psalm 98 also reveals that:

> *"HaShem has made known His salvation before the eyes of the nations, He has revealed His righteousness.*
>
> Psalm 98:2

The question that must be asked is how has G-d made known this salvation to the nations (Gentiles)? The answer is found in the next verse:

> *"Remember His grace and His faithfulness to the House of Israel; See O all the ends of the earth the salvation of our G-d."*
>
> Psalm 98:3

In other words, **HaShem has revealed to the nations His salvation by the grace and faithfulness that He demonstrated to the House of Israel.** One needs to remember that this

Psalm relates to the Kingdom. The implications of this are that when the Gentiles witness G-d acting in light of His covenant promises to the Jewish people, they will be moved to respond to His salvation message. This Biblical truth has been seen in numerous other passages which have already been studied in this work. The Psalm ends with a statement concerning the purpose for why Messiah has established His Kingdom:

> "*Before HaShem, for He has come to judge the earth, He will judge the world in righteousness and peoples with uprightness.*"
>
> Psalm 98:9

This verse begins with the phrase, "*Before HaShem.*" These words imply that what Messiah Yeshua has come to do is indeed proper according to G-d's will. Most English translations either place this verse in the present or future tense. That is, Yeshua is coming or will come. The Hebrew verb is אב, and it can be understood in the present tense or the past tense. Context, however, seems to imply that Yeshua has already come and the purpose of the verse is to simply state why He has come. The reason is for judgment. Judgment is an important aspect of Yeshua's work in the Millennial Kingdom. However, judgment will not at all be present in the New Jerusalem (judgment will not be necessary, as the New Jerusalem will represent a state of perfection).

There are, in fact, several Scriptural distinctions between the Millennial Kingdom and the New Jerusalem. Those theologians who fail to discern these differences, likewise fail to discern many of the unique characteristics of the Millennium. This leads such theologians to deny the Millennial Kingdom altogether or to combine the Millennium and the New Jerusalem into one Kingdom.

In conclusion, the Millennial Kingdom represents an important part of HaShem's divine plan in establishing THE KINGDOM! In this usage, the term "THE KINGDOM" represents the final and eternal state of G-d's Kingdom, known as the New Jerusalem. Throughout this study of the key Scriptural passages related to the Millennium, it has been demonstrated time and time again how every piece of information contained in the Biblical text is vital, in order to assist the reader in arriving at a proper understanding of the Millennial Kingdom. Those who are forced to spiritualize and allegorize these texts in order to maintain their theological positions, actually miss out on seeing how true G-d is to His word and the great continuity between the Old and New Covenants.

For those who embrace the Scriptural reality of a Millennial Kingdom, which is taught in many of the prophetic writings, there is a clear and encouraging message of the fidelity of G-d to His covenant promises. This fidelity, when it is received by Israel in the last days, will be a great source of evangelism, which will bring exceedingly many Gentiles to faith in Messiah Yeshua. If one is truly interested in Gentiles coming to faith in the Gospel, then the Millennial Kingdom will be of great importance to such an individual.

Epilogue

ENTRANCE INTO THE KINGDOM

Perhaps **you** have heard of the phrase "The Gospel," but the majority of the people in the world have not. This word is Hebrew in origin and relates to **the good news about redemption**. Redemption is a word which has an accounting application to it and involves a change in ownership. In simple terms, the Gospel involves a payment which causes that which was redeemed to become the possession of another. Humanity, ever since the first sin, has been ruled over by sin. In other words, sin owned man and man was without hope. This hopelessness was due to the fact that humanity was unable to free itself from the power and bondage of sin. By means of G-d's revelation to man (Scripture), man learned of his need for a Redeemer or Saviour.

The Prophets revealed that the One who would do the work of redemption and offer to humanity the opportunity to be saved, i.e. to have one's sins forgiven, would be known as the Messiah or the Anointed One (The Christ). The Scriptures also linked the word "Gospel" to the Messiah. It is most significant that the Hebrew word for the Gospel is הרושבה which is derived from the same Hebrew word which means "**flesh.**" In the verbal form this word means "to proclaim the good news concerning redemption." The fact that the same Hebrew root is used for both has caused scholars to ask the question, "*What is the relationship between proclaiming the message of redemption and the term flesh?*" The answer is that G-d has entered into this world in the flesh by means of the Messiah, in order to redeem mankind.

When examining the Biblical record, it is clear that the Word of G-d reveals that Yeshua (Jesus) of Nazareth is indeed the Messiah. It is by His death on the tree and the shedding of His blood that the work of redemption was fulfilled, **once and for all**. In order to underscore that Yeshua is the Redeemer, His death occurred on the fourteenth day of the Jewish month of Nissan, or on the day that the Passover sacrifice was offered. Passover is known as the festival of redemption. How should one respond to Yeshua in order that he or she shall be saved?

Below is a list of 7 things which one must confess and/or believe in order to find personal redemption.

1. To confess that you are a sinner and do not have a personal relationship with the Living G-d. Isaiah 59:1-2 states, "*Behold, the hand of the L-rd is not so short that He cannot save, nor is His ear too heavy from hearing, rather your iniquities separate you from G-d and your sins have caused His face to be hidden from hearing.*"

2. To confess before G-d that you do not want to continue to sin.

3. To confess before G-d that you are unable to save yourself.

4. To confess before G-d that you acknowledge that Yeshua was sent by G-d the Father to be your Passover sacrifice, when He died upon the tree.

5. To believe that Yeshua from Nazareth is Messiah and only through faith in Him is one redeemed/saved.

6. To believe that Yeshua's blood was shed for the remission of sins and established the New Covenant of which Jeremiah chapter 31 spoke.

7. To believe that Yeshua rose from the dead on the third day as the Scriptures state.

The following is a sample prayer that one may pray in order to find personal redemption by means of the grace of G-d:

*I confess before you, O G-d, that I am a sinner. I confess that I am not able to save myself. Therefore I turn to Yeshua from Nazareth, Your only Begotten Son, Whom You sent into this world to redeem me. I believe that He died upon the tree (cross) in order for all my sins to be forgiven. I believe that He rose from the dead, signifying the victory over sin that He **offers** to all who believe in Him. I believe that only through His blood that You forgive my sin, those which I have committed and will commit in the future. I want to invite You, Yeshua, to be my L-rd, send me Your Holy Spirit, that I might walk in Your ways, obeying Your Word, in the Name of Yeshua the Messiah, Amen.*

When you pray this prayer or one similar to it, Scripture promises that your name is written in the Lamb's (Yeshua's) *Book of Life*. The implication of this fact is that you will be part of G-d's eternal Kingdom. Praise Yeshua that our salvation is not dependent upon our works, but solely upon His work of redemption on the Cross and the evidence of this salvation is the fact that G-d raised Yeshua from the dead.

Amen.

For more information of R. Baruch's Hebrew ministry,
please visit

www.pdut.org

Or if you would like to hear more of R. Baruch's teaching
in English, visit

www.LoveIsrael.org